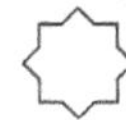

THIS COLORING BOOK

BELONG TO :

TRYING AREA

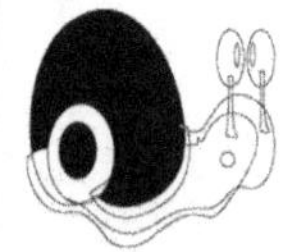

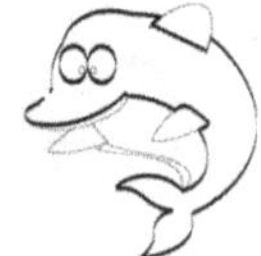

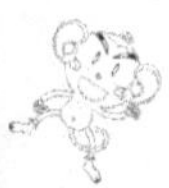
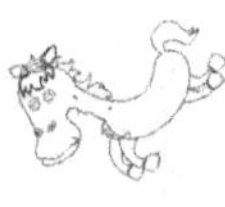
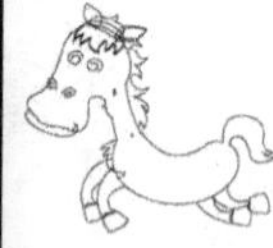

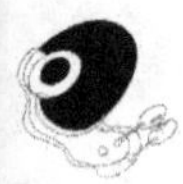
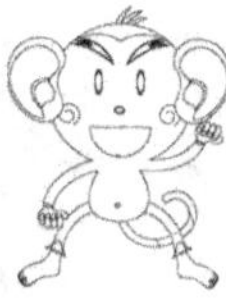
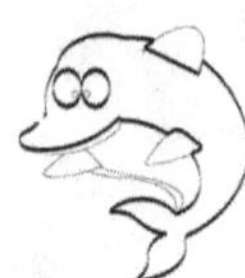
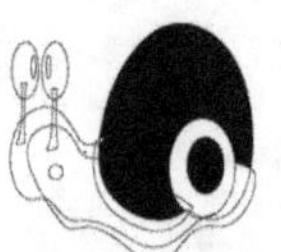

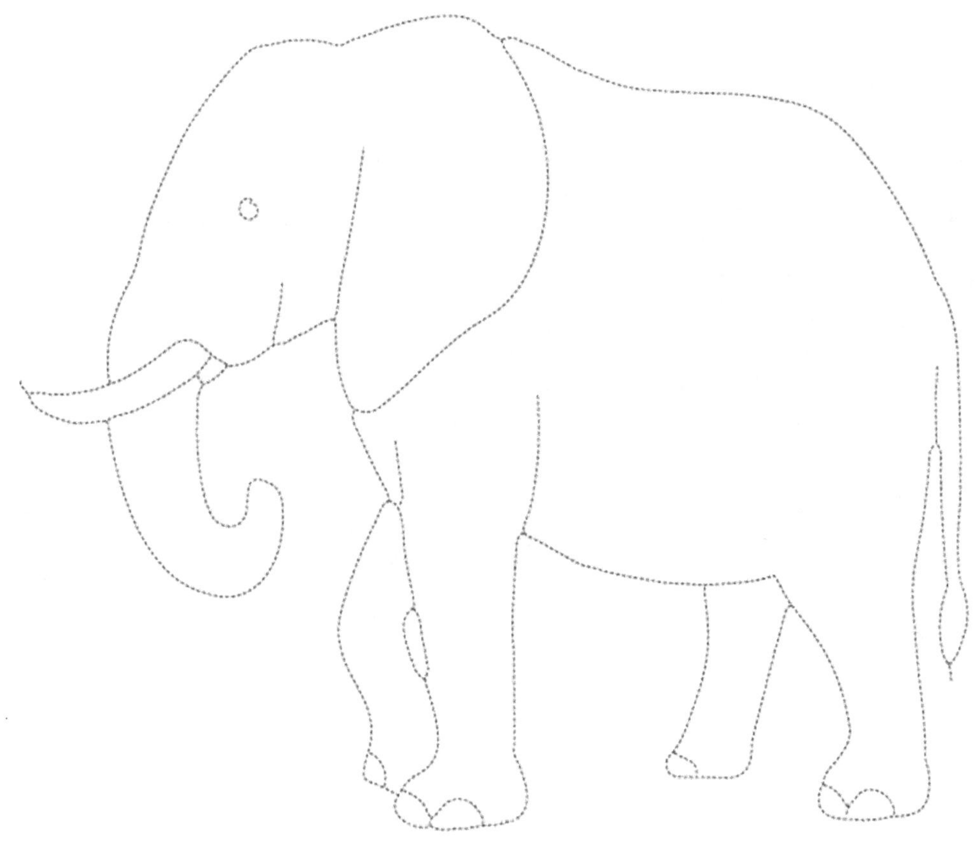

Elephant

TRYING AREA

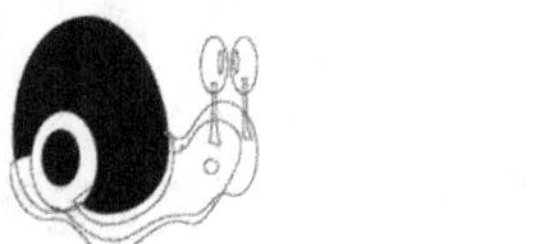

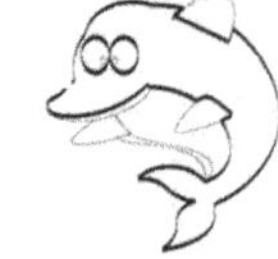

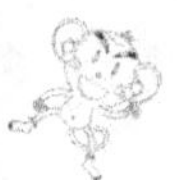
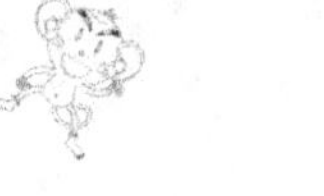
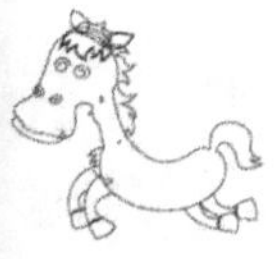
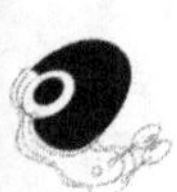
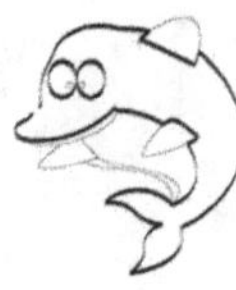
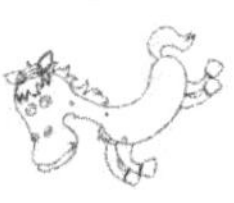

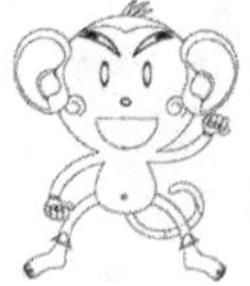
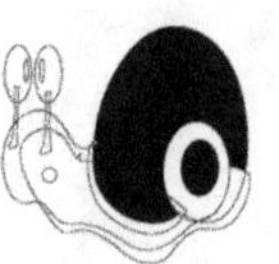

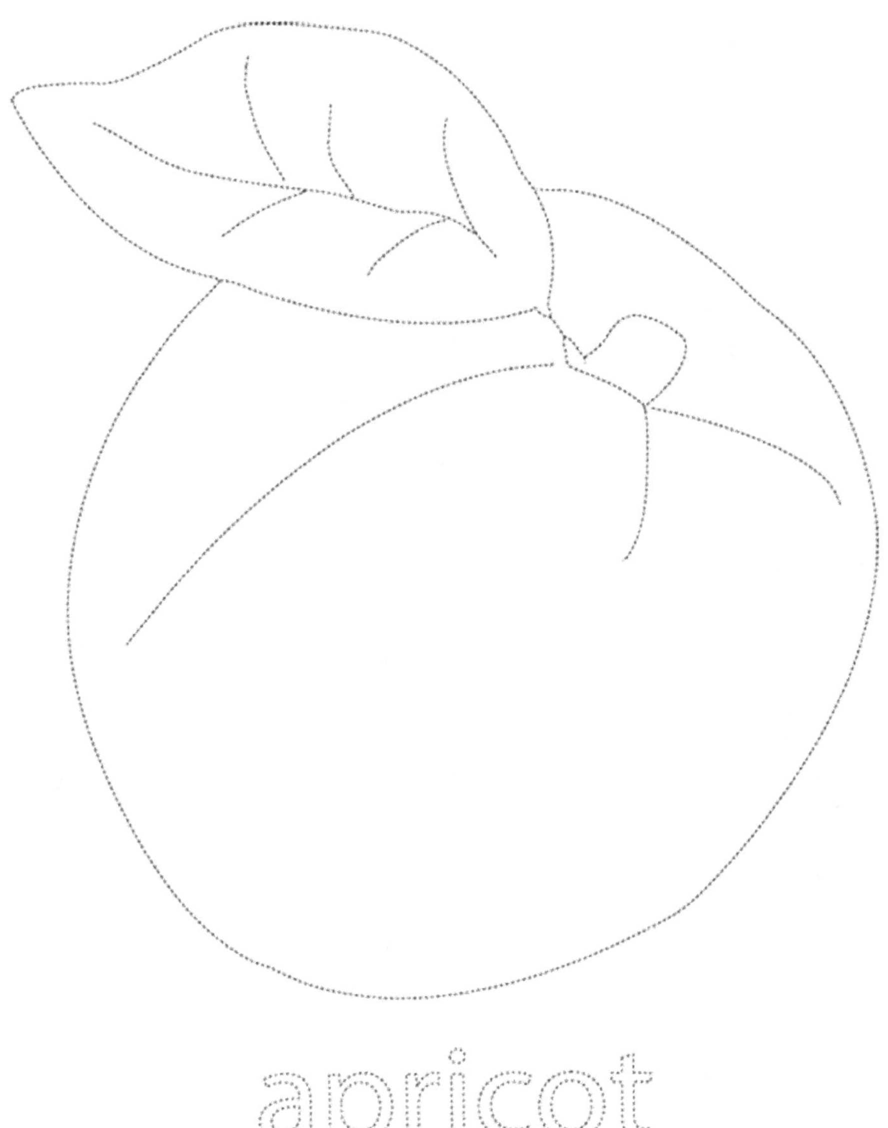

apricot

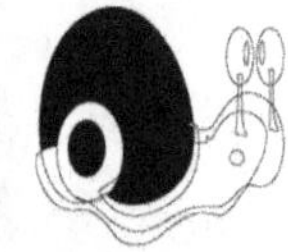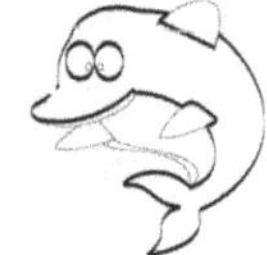

TRYING AREA

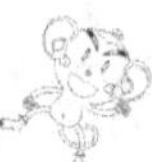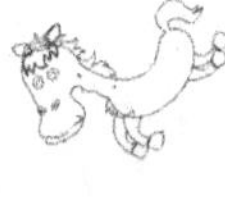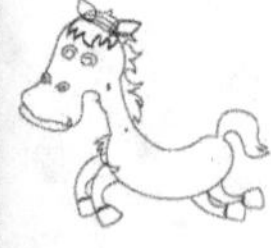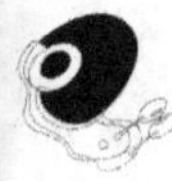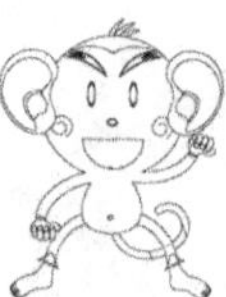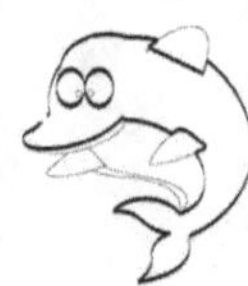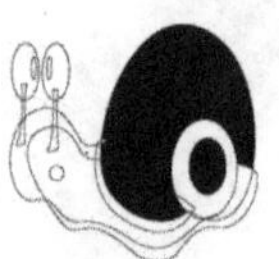

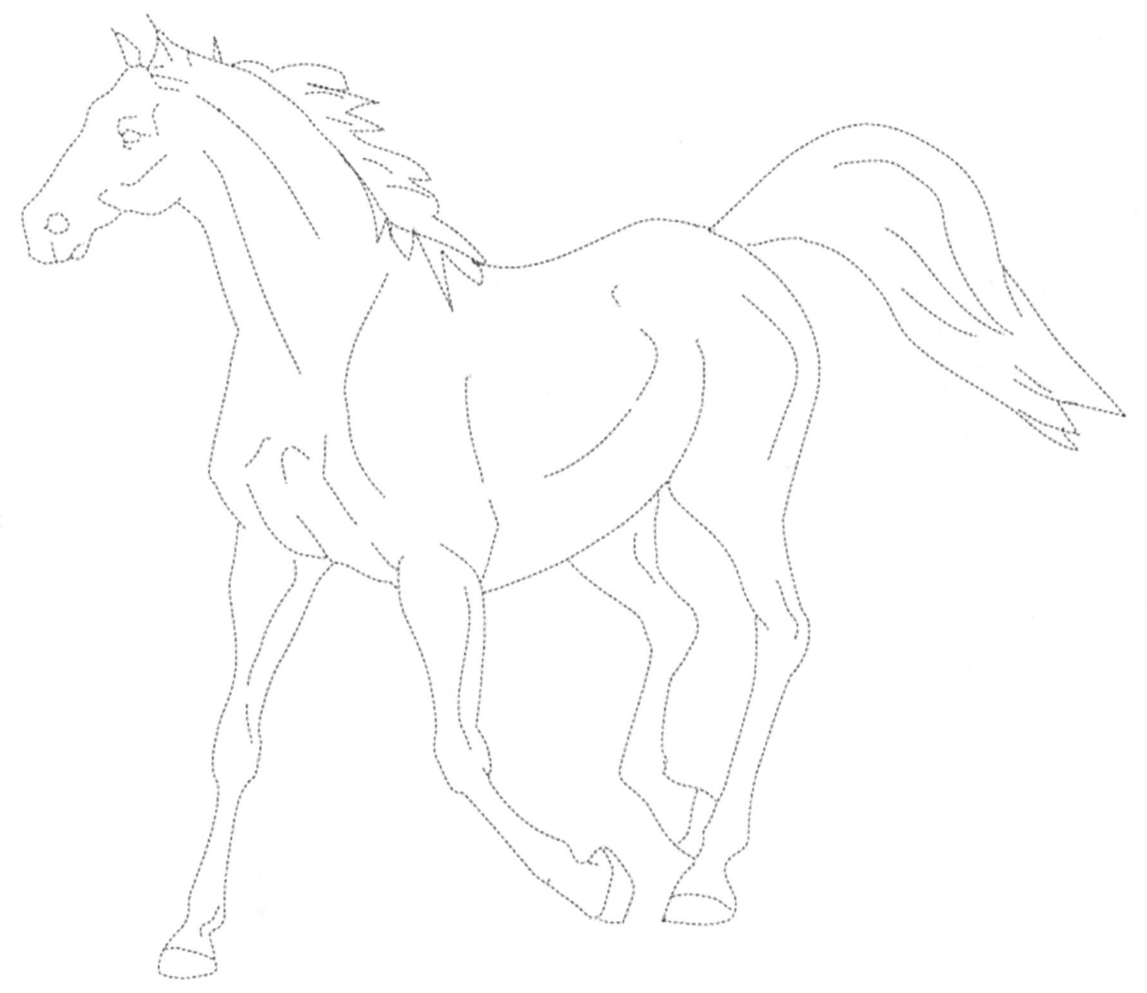

Horse

TRYING AREA

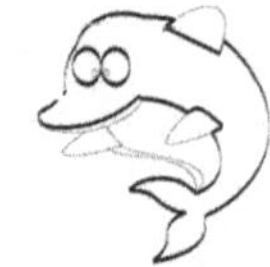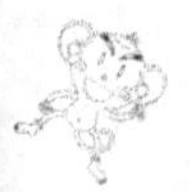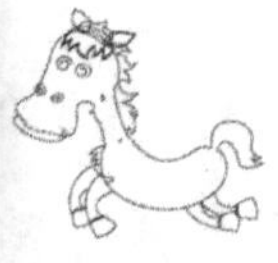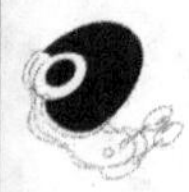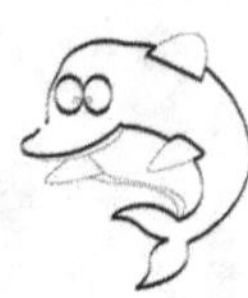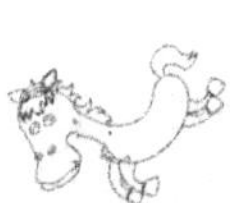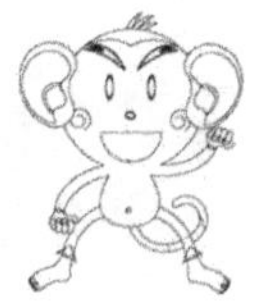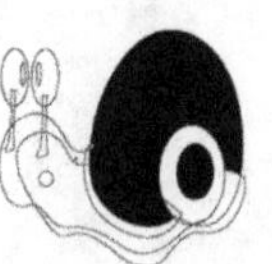

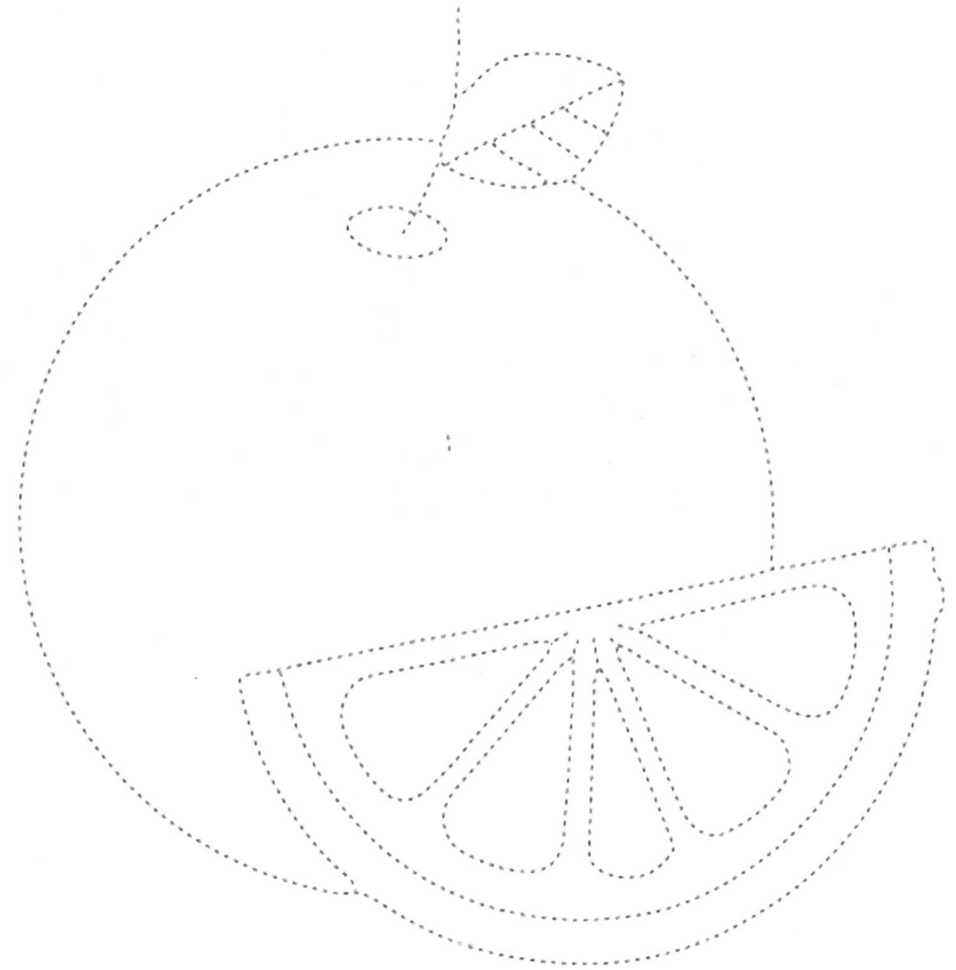

grapefruit

TRYING AREA

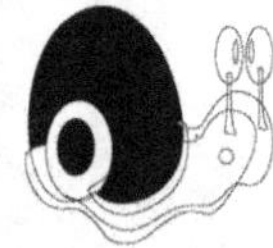

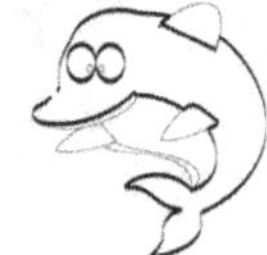

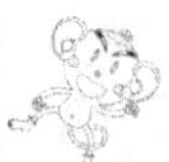
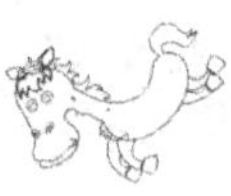

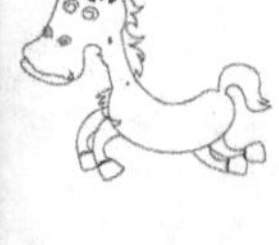

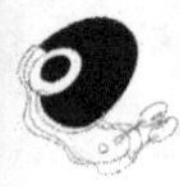
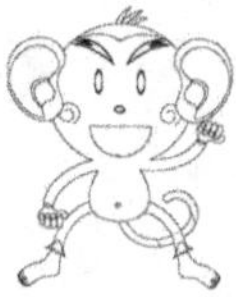
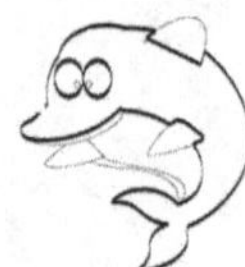
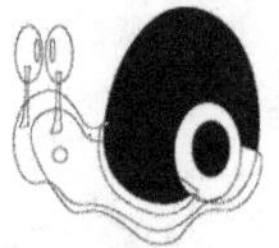

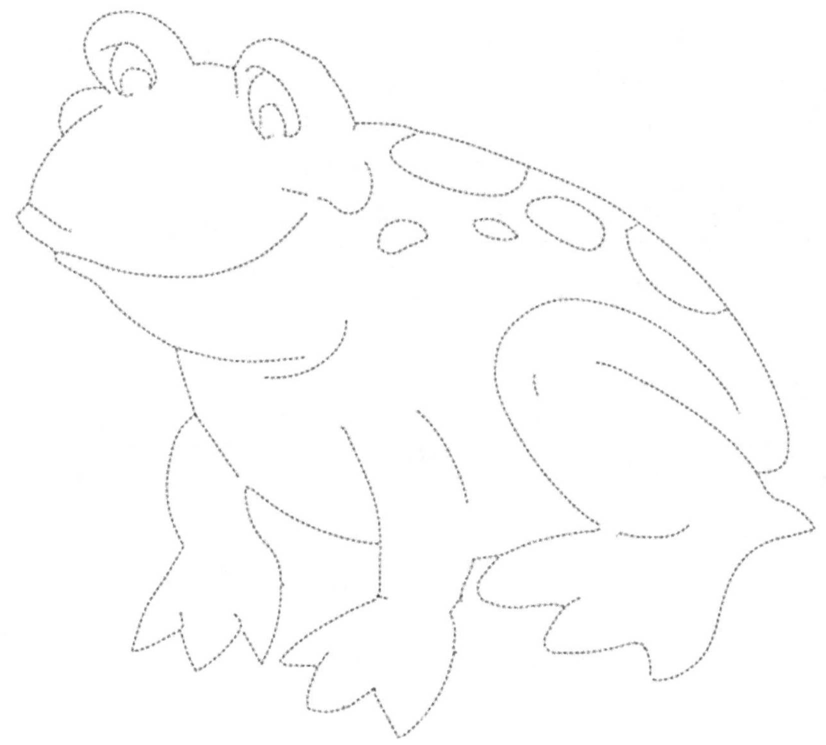

Frog

TRYING AREA

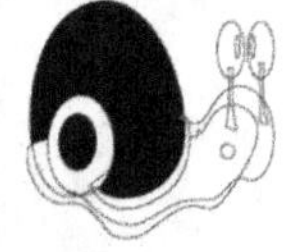
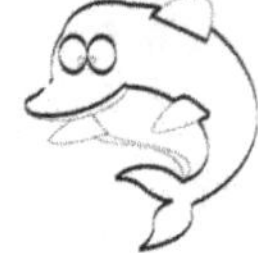

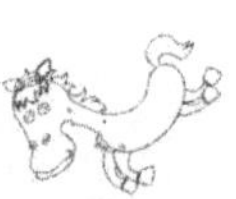
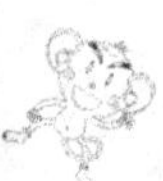

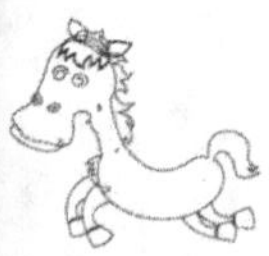
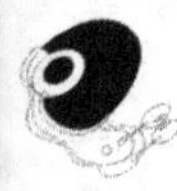
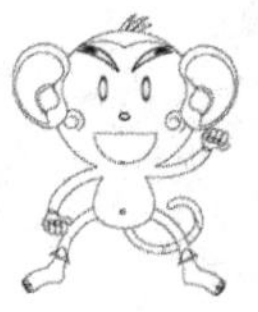
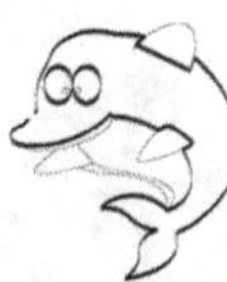
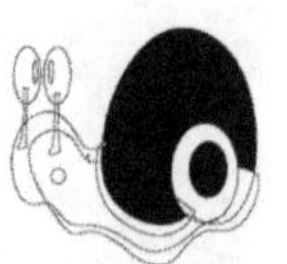

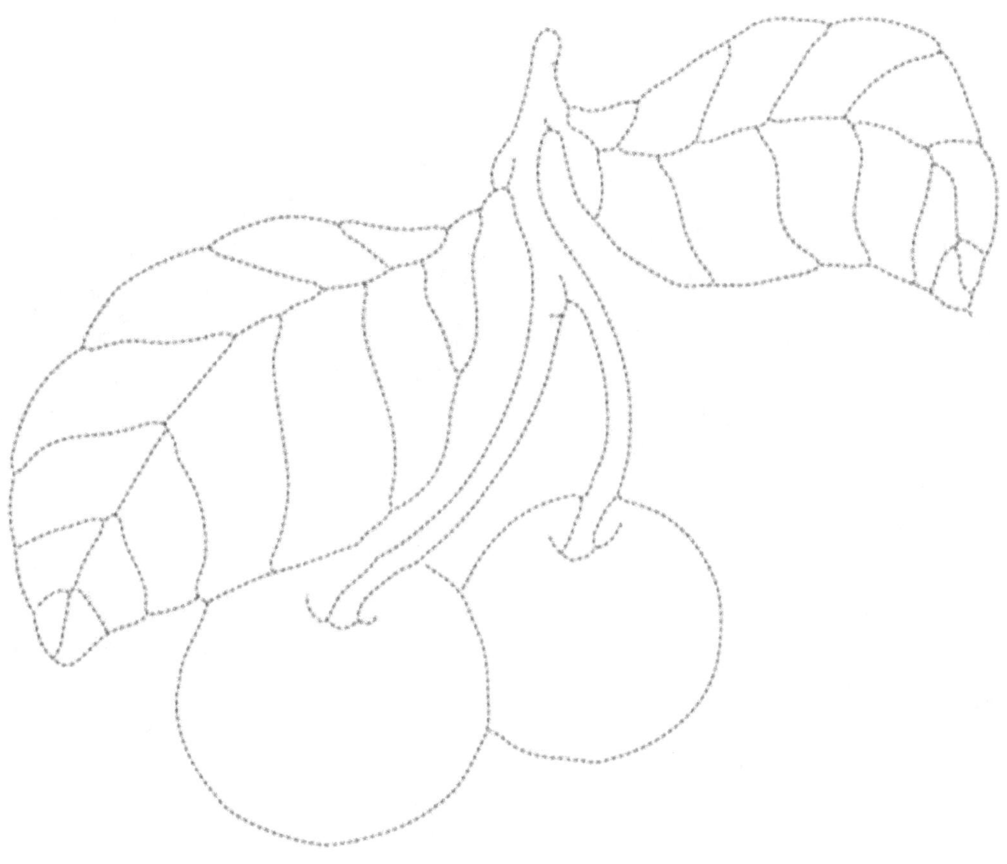

cherry

TRYING AREA

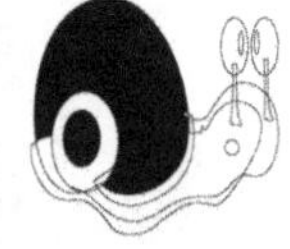

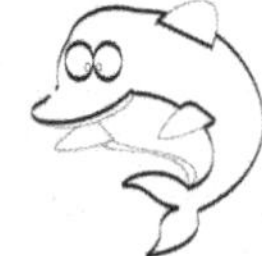

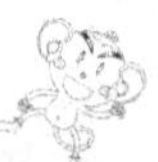
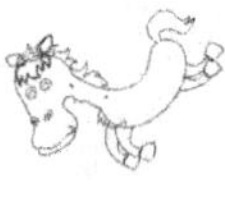
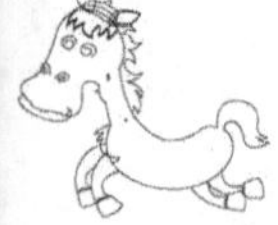

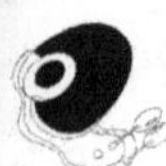
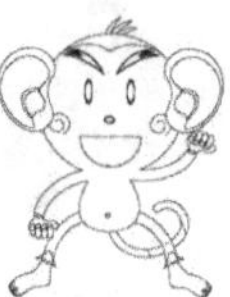
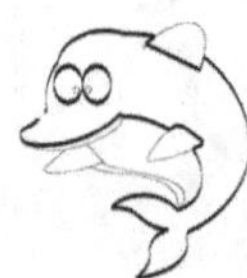
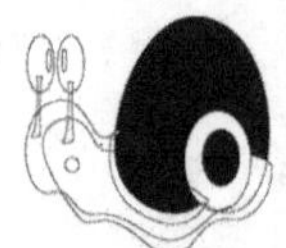

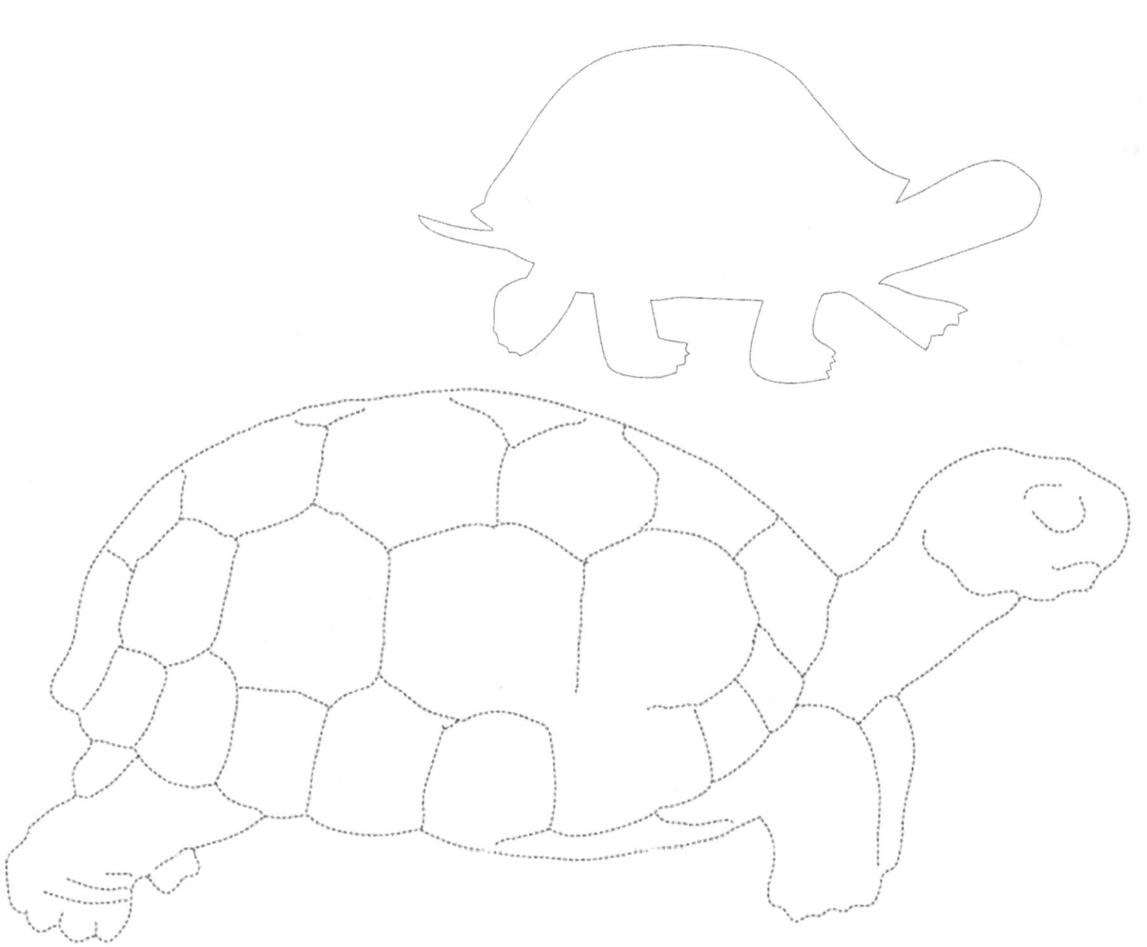

Turtle

TRYING AREA

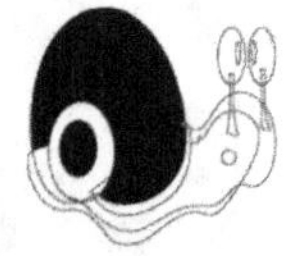

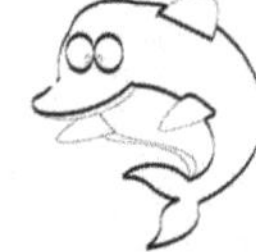

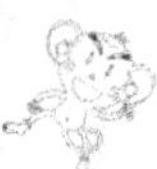
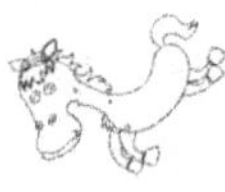
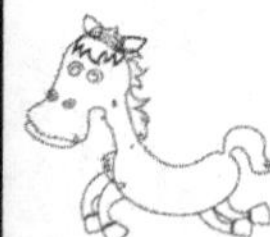

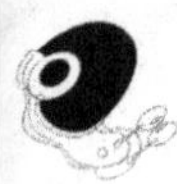
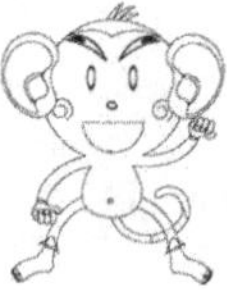
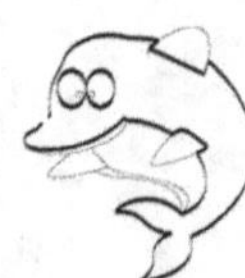
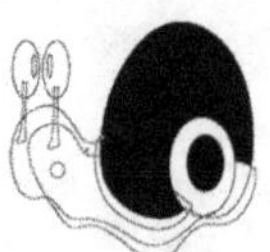

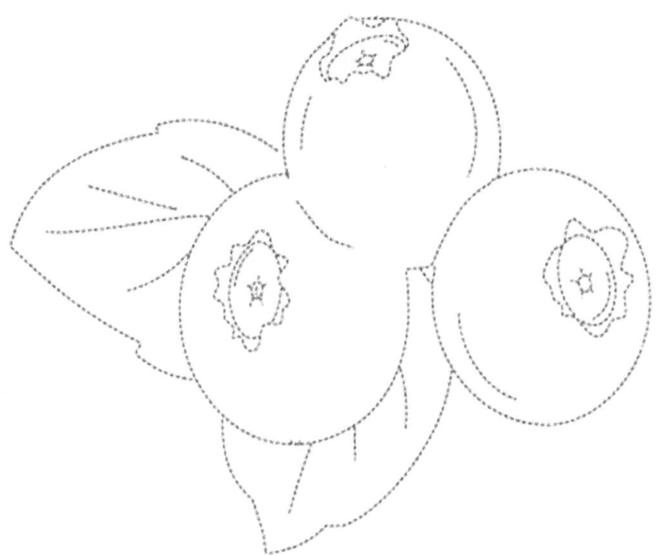

Blueberry

TRYING AREA

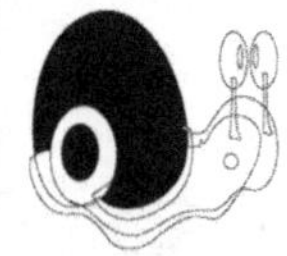

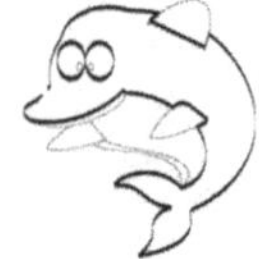

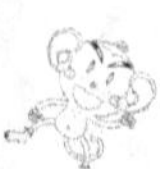
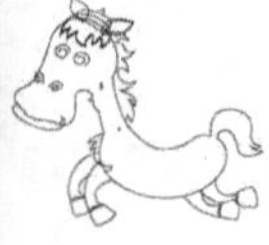
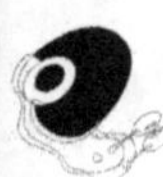
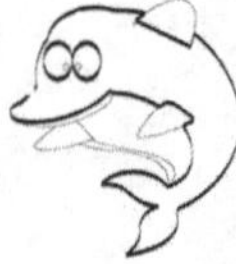
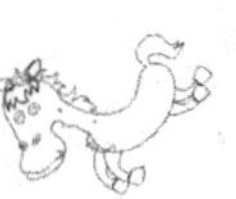

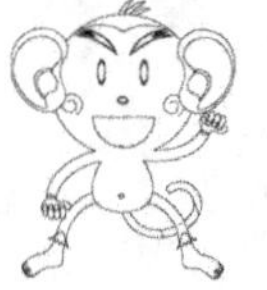
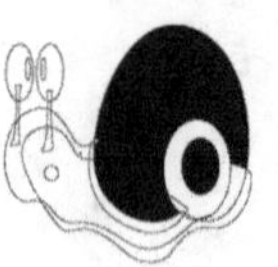

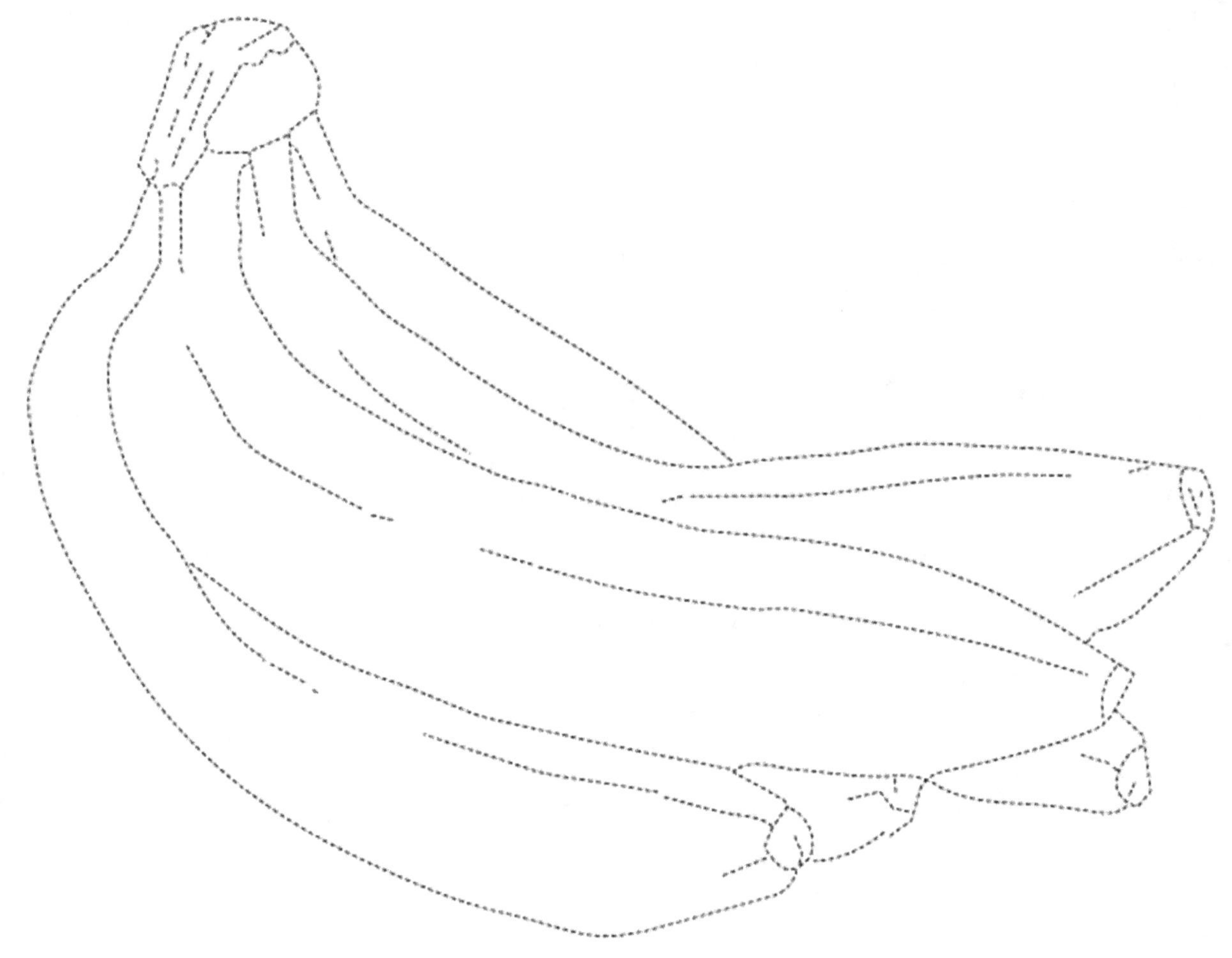

bananas

TRYING AREA

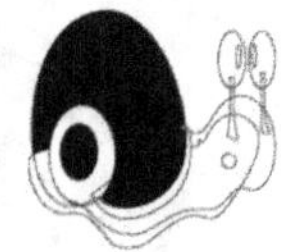

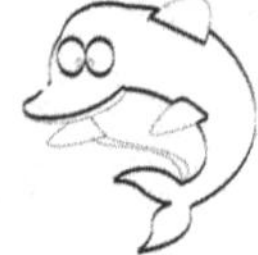

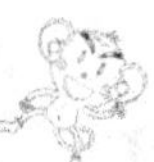
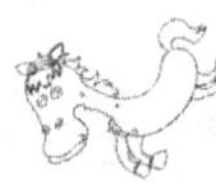
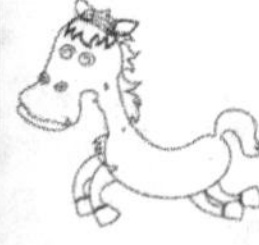

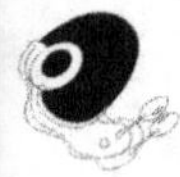
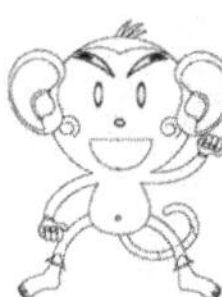
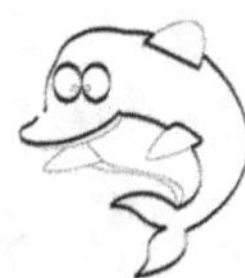
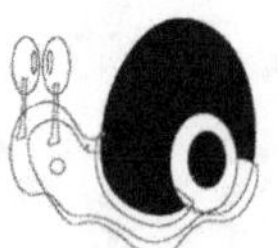

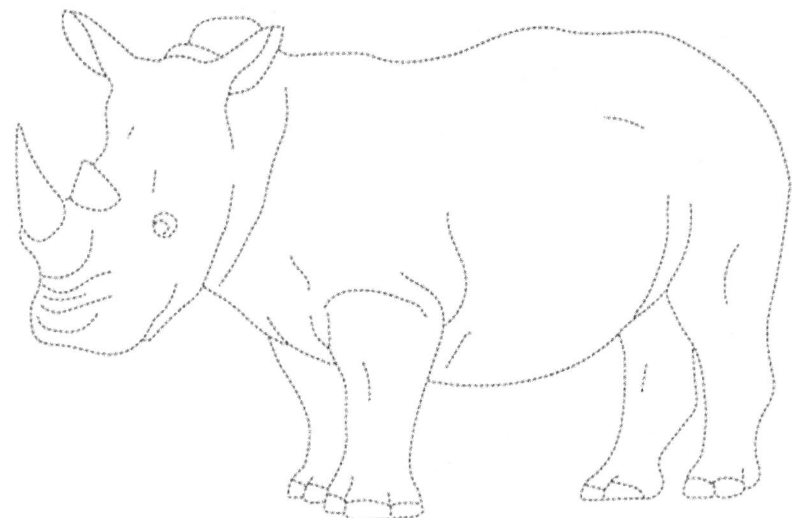

Rhino

TRYING AREA

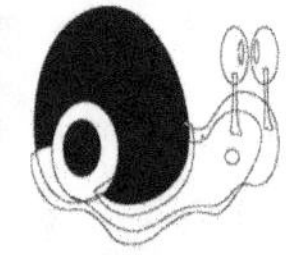

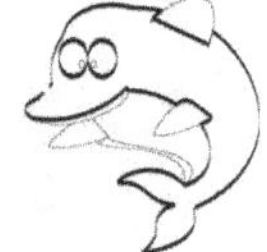

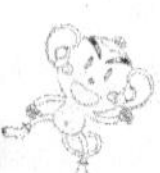
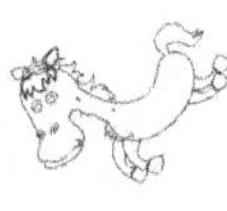
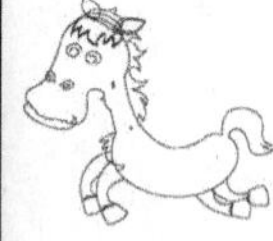

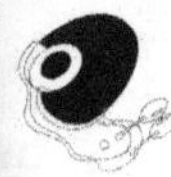
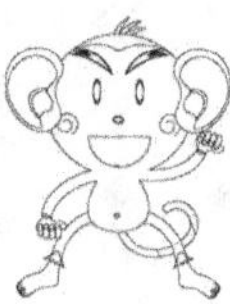
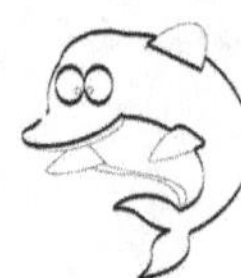
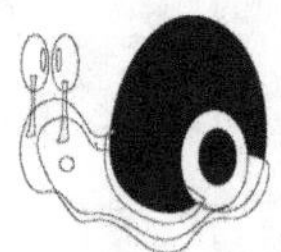

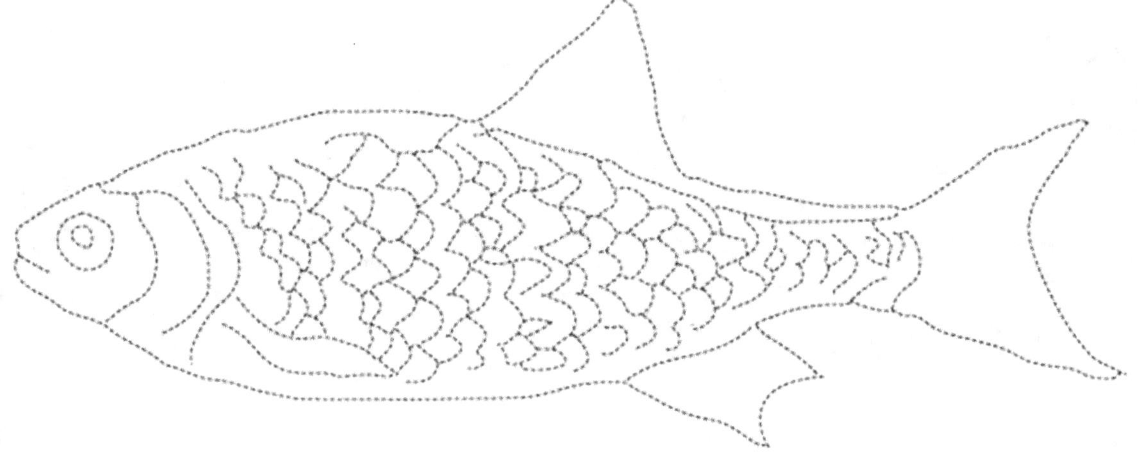

Fish

TRYING AREA

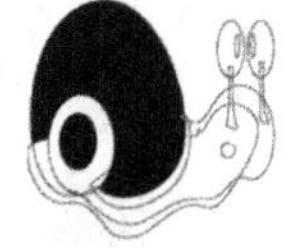

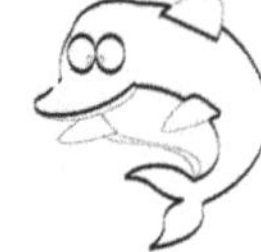

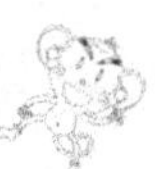
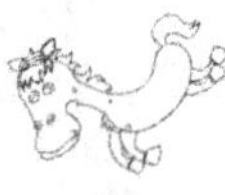
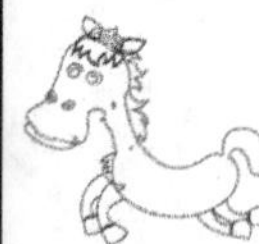

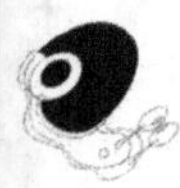
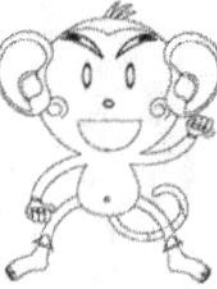
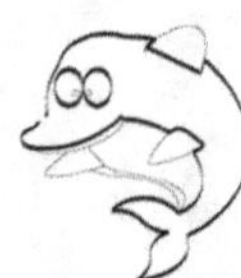
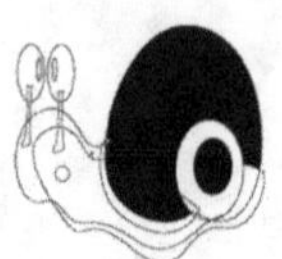

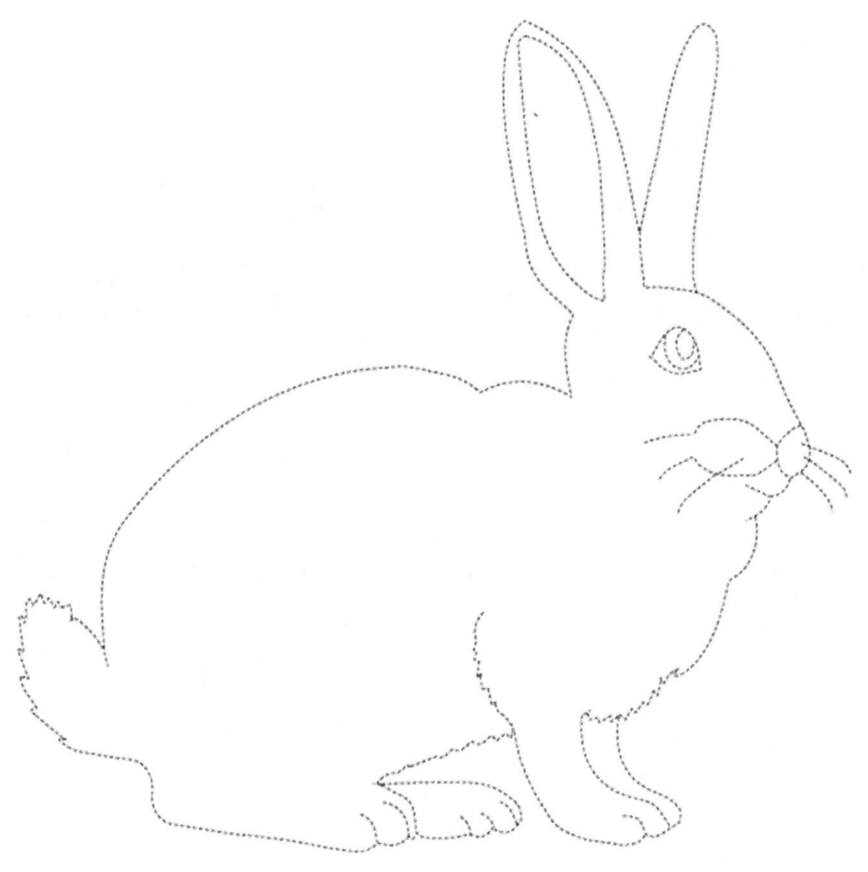

Rabbit

TRYING AREA

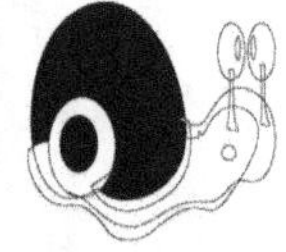

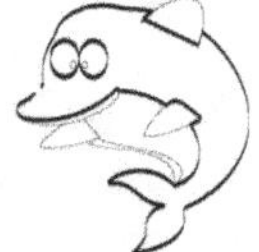

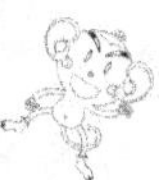
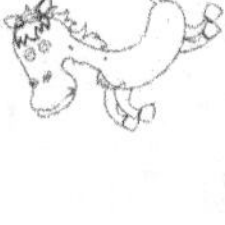
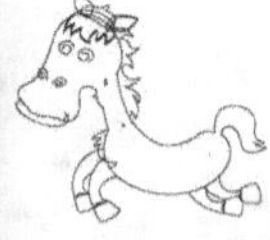

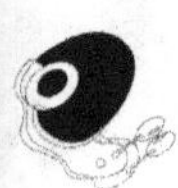
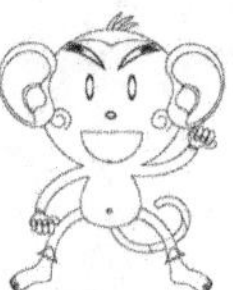
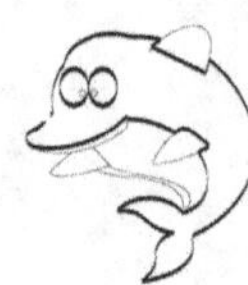
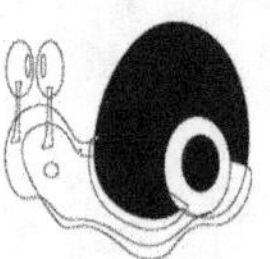

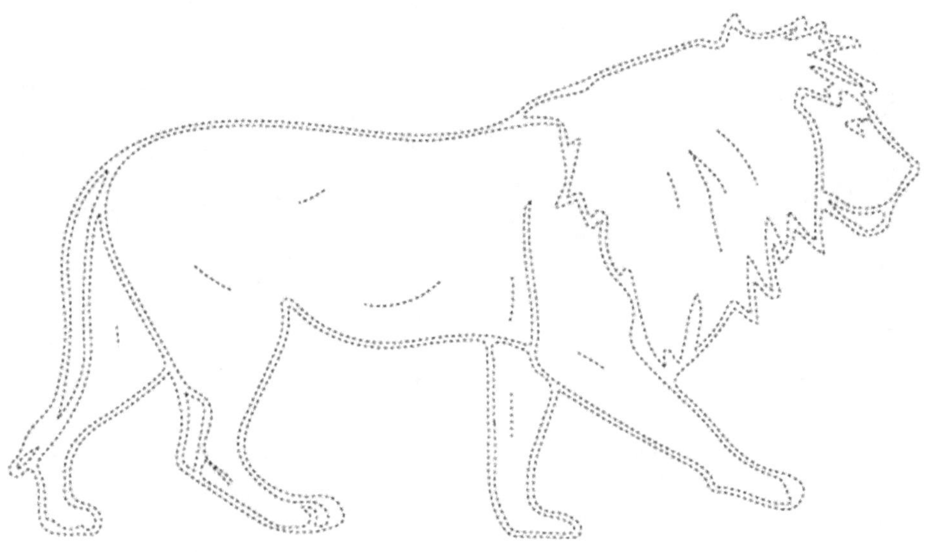

Lion

TRYING AREA

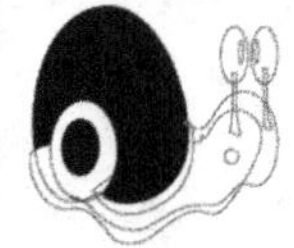

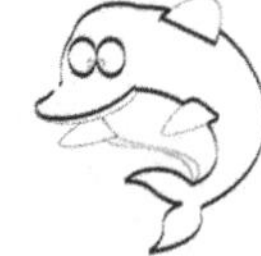

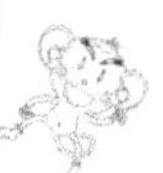
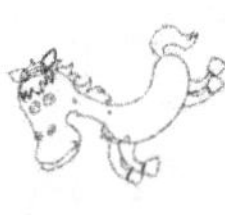
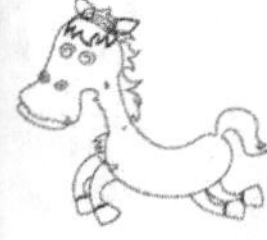

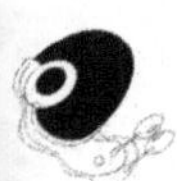
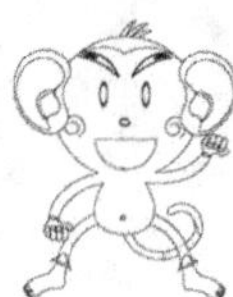
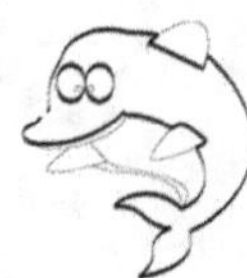
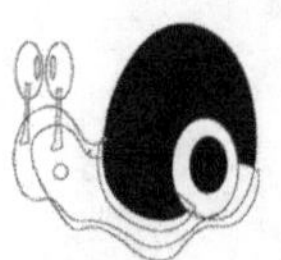

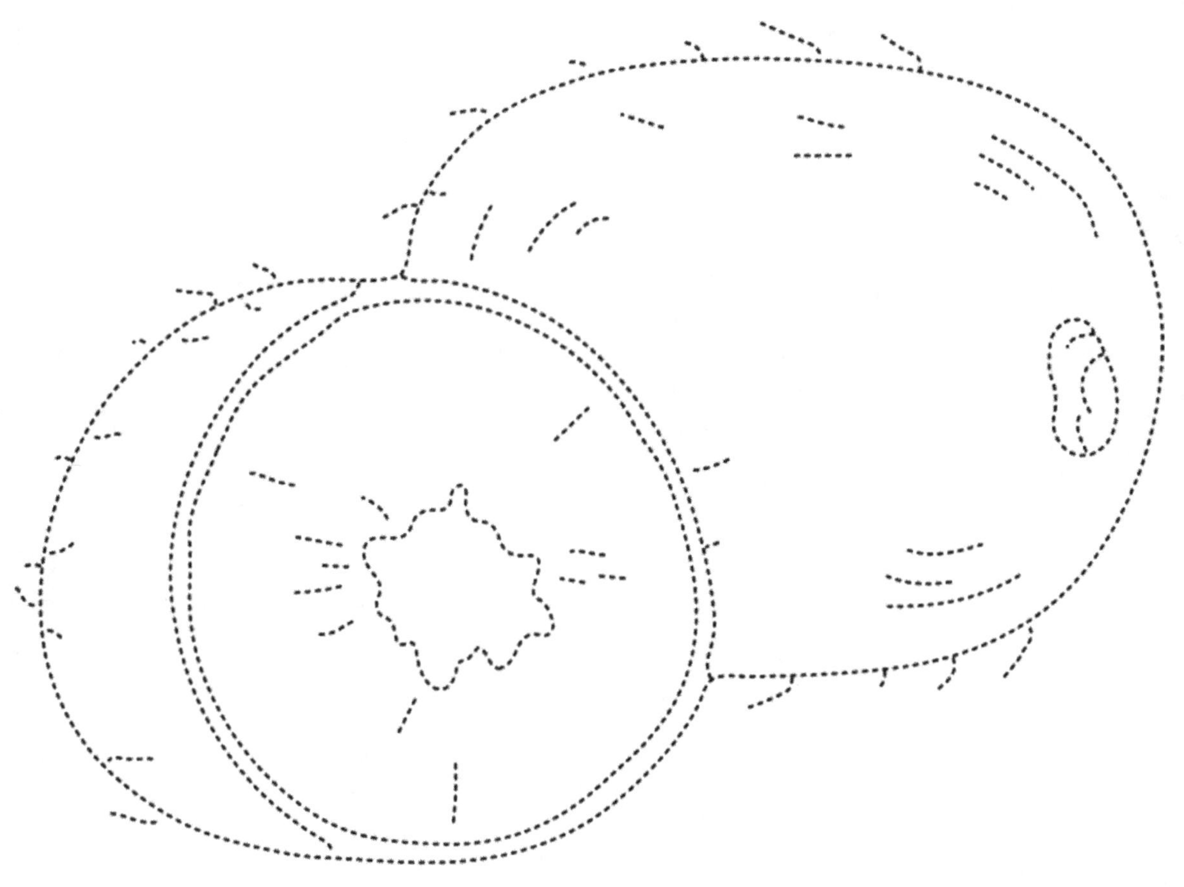

kiwi

TRYING AREA

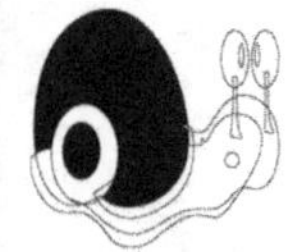

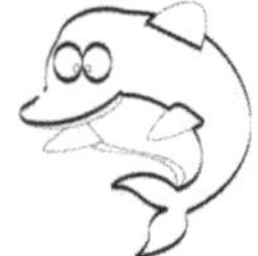

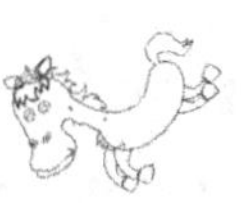
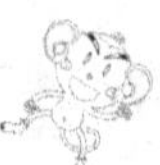

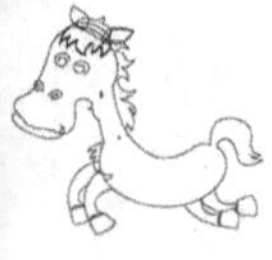
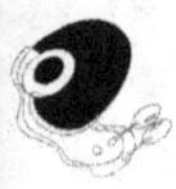
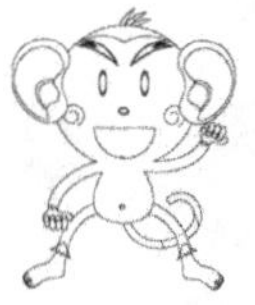
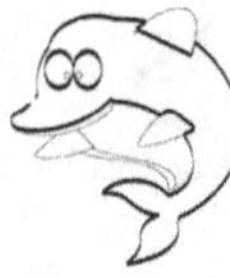
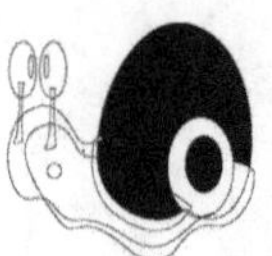

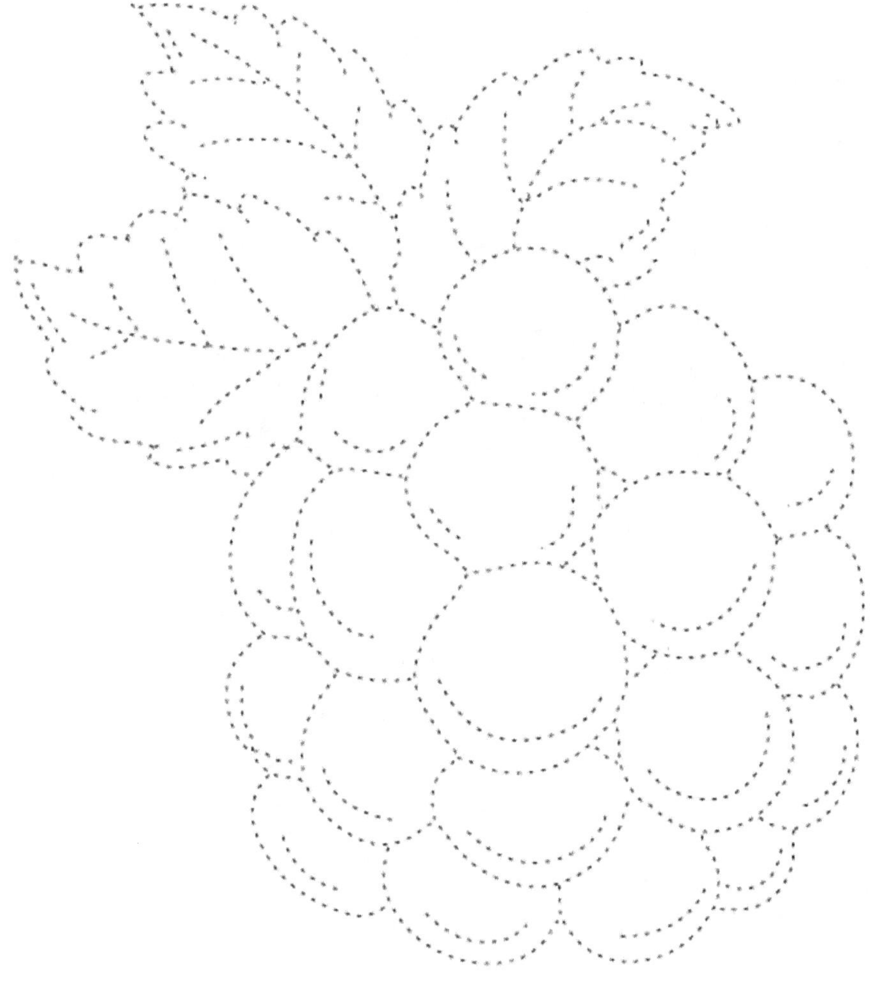

blackberry

TRYING AREA

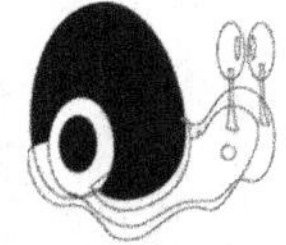

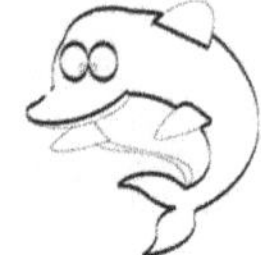

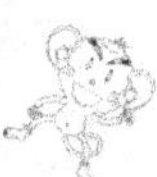
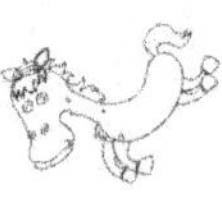
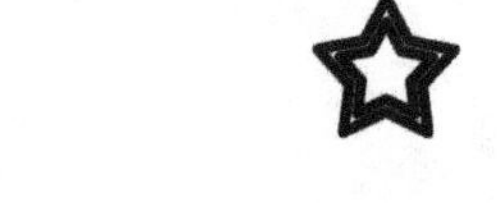
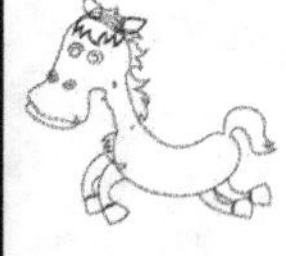
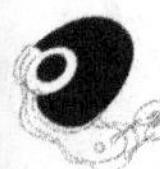
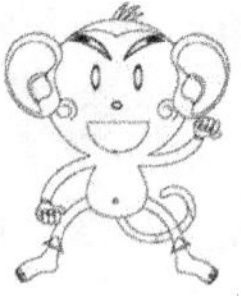
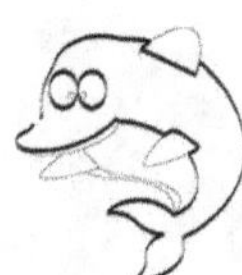
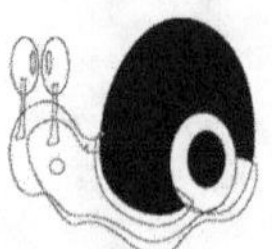

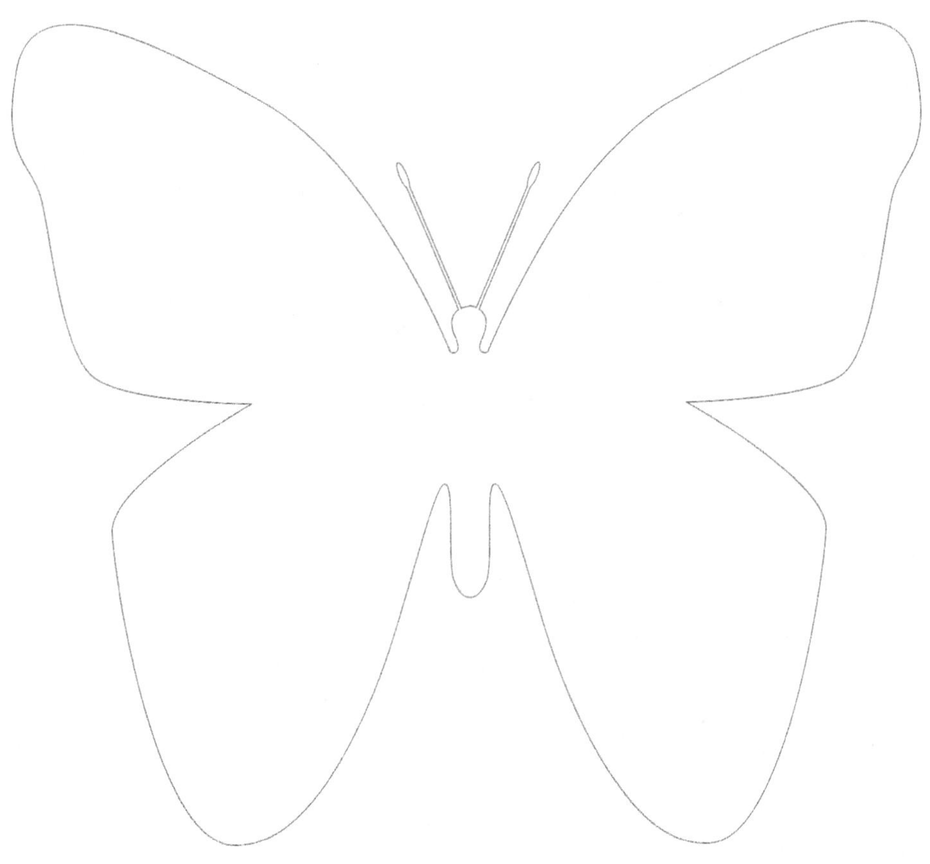

Butterfly

TRYING AREA

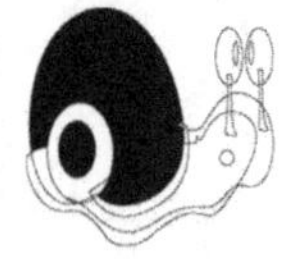

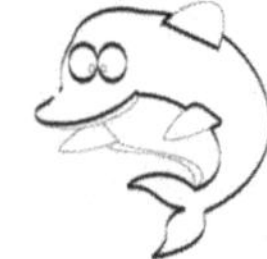

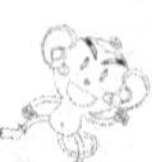
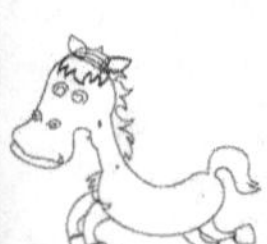
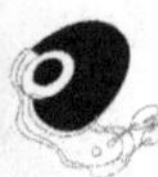
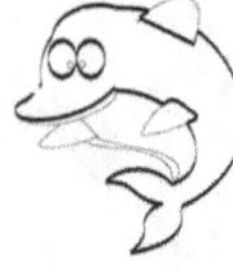
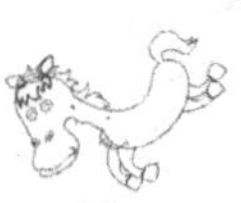

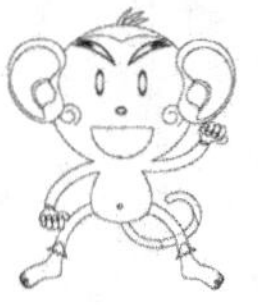
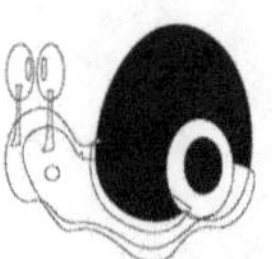

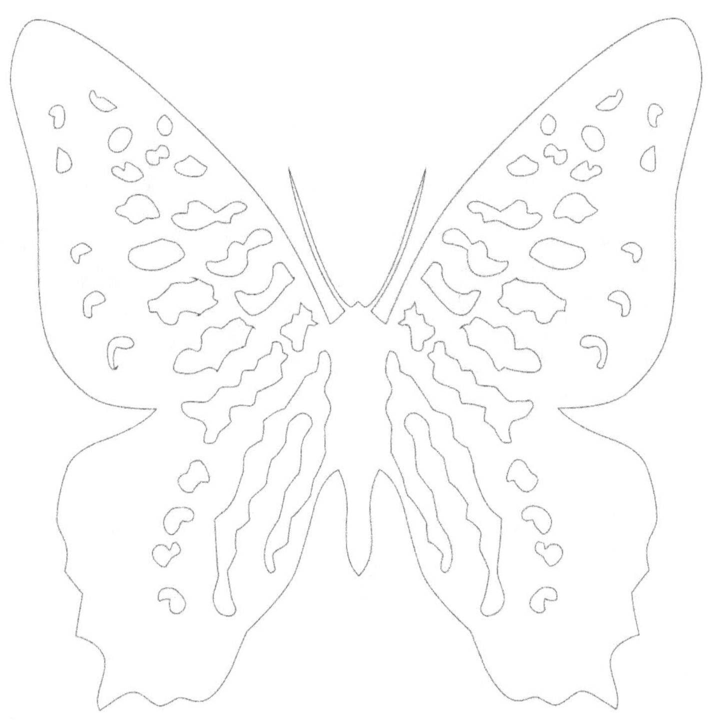

ButterMoth

TRYING AREA

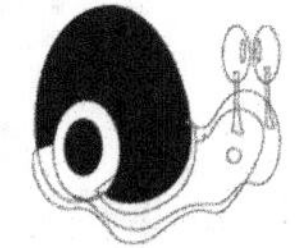

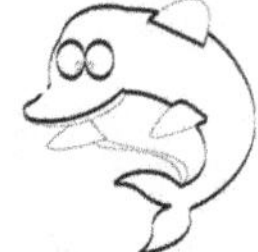

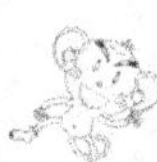
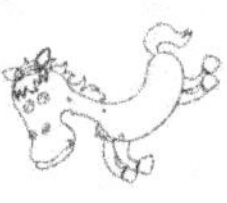

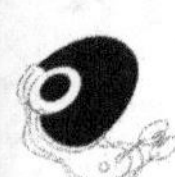
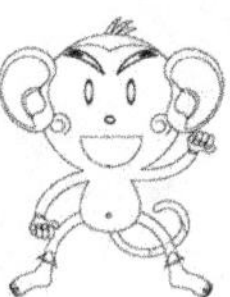
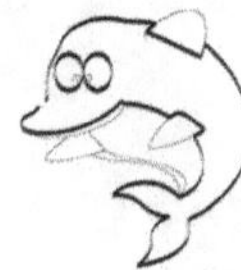
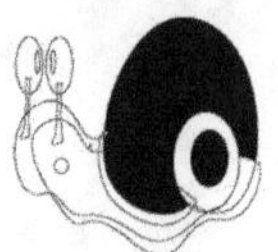

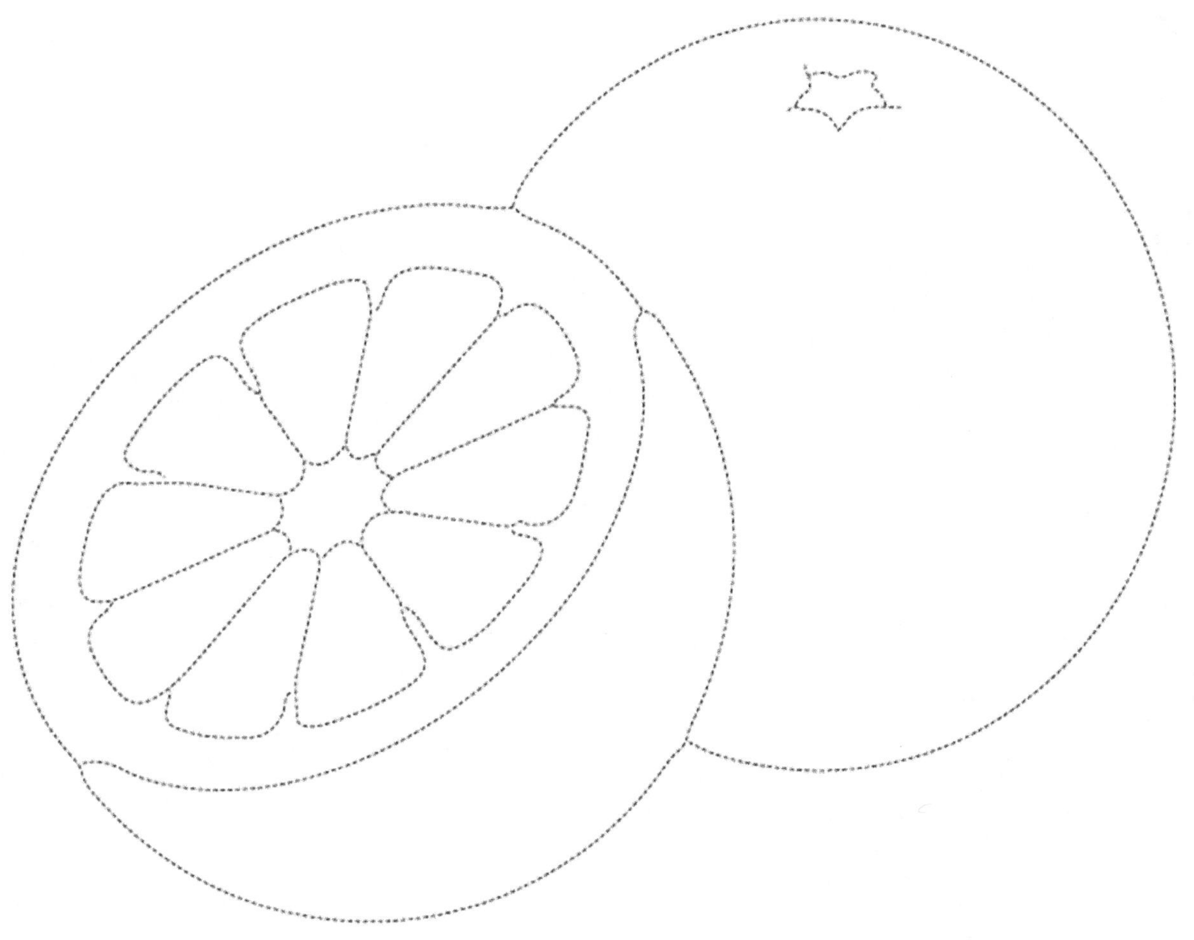

orange

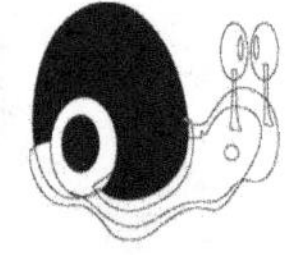

TRYING AREA

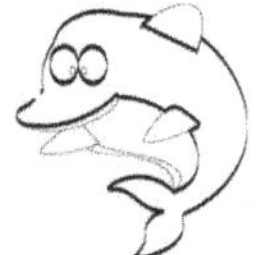

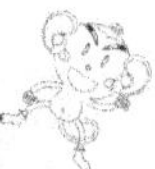
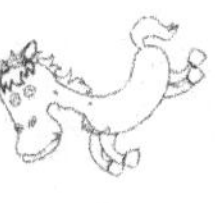
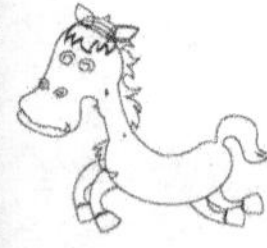

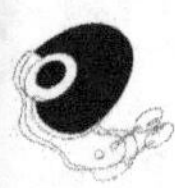
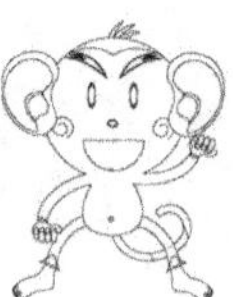
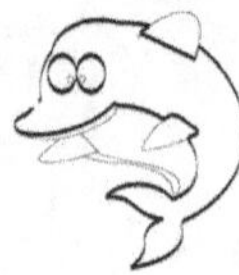
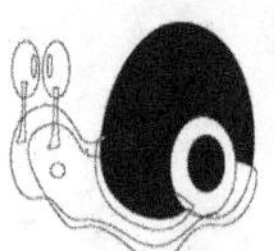

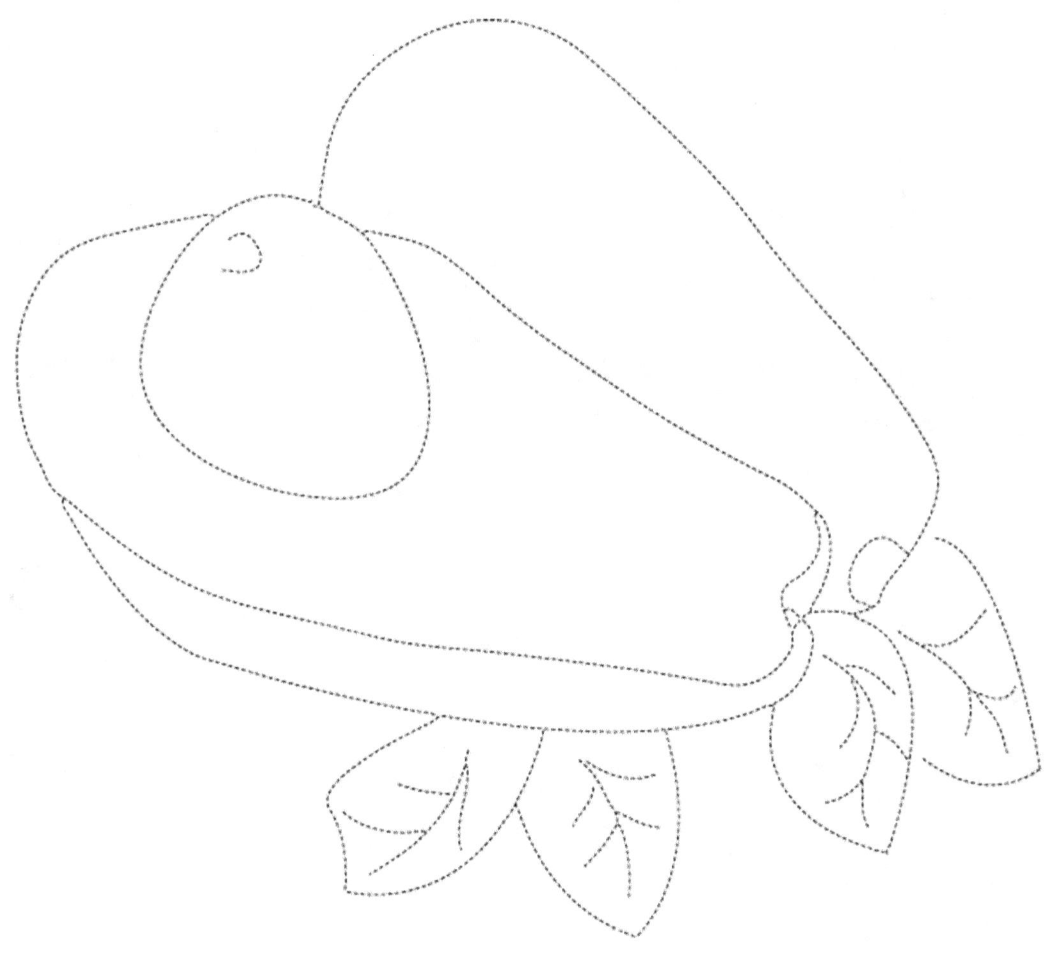

avocado

TRYING AREA

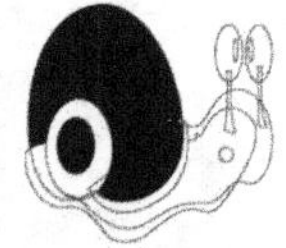
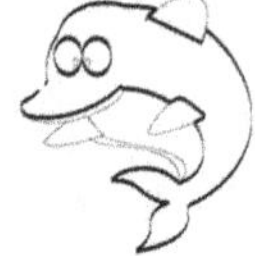

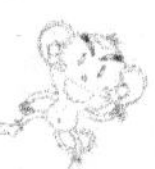
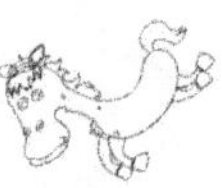

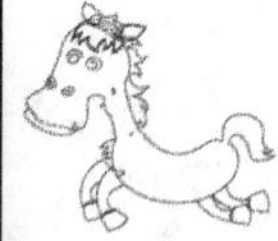
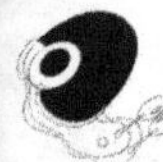
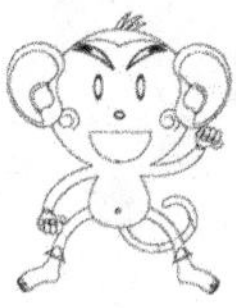
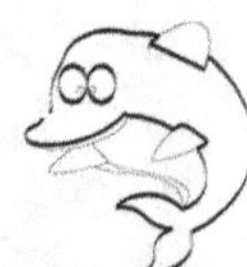
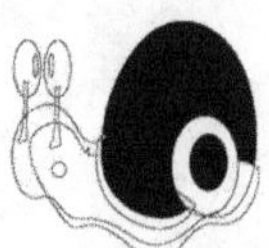

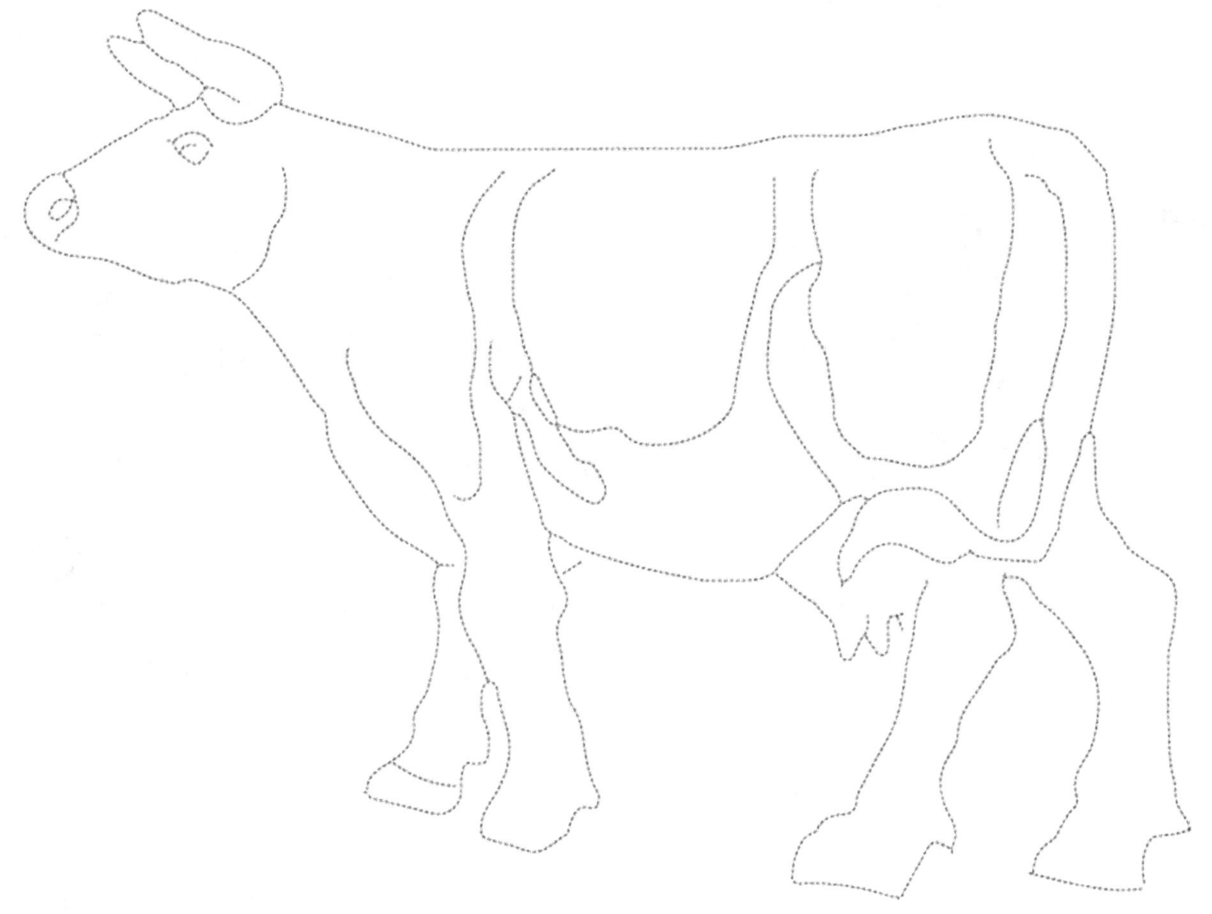

Cow

TRYING AREA

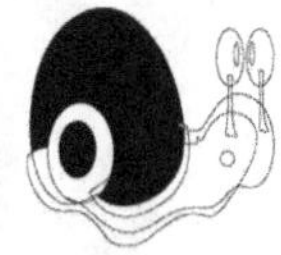

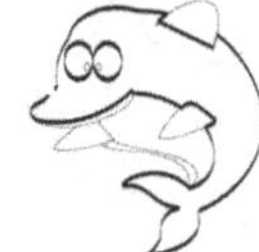

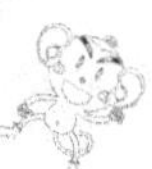
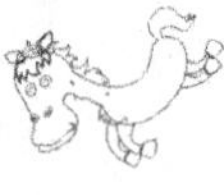
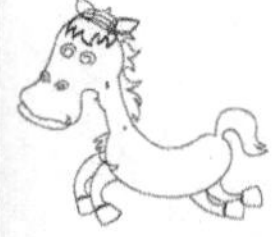

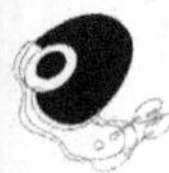
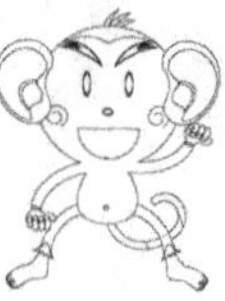
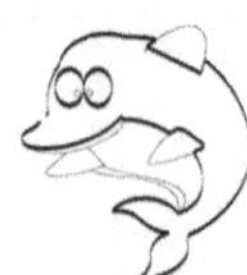
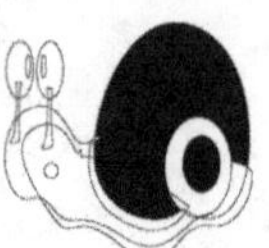

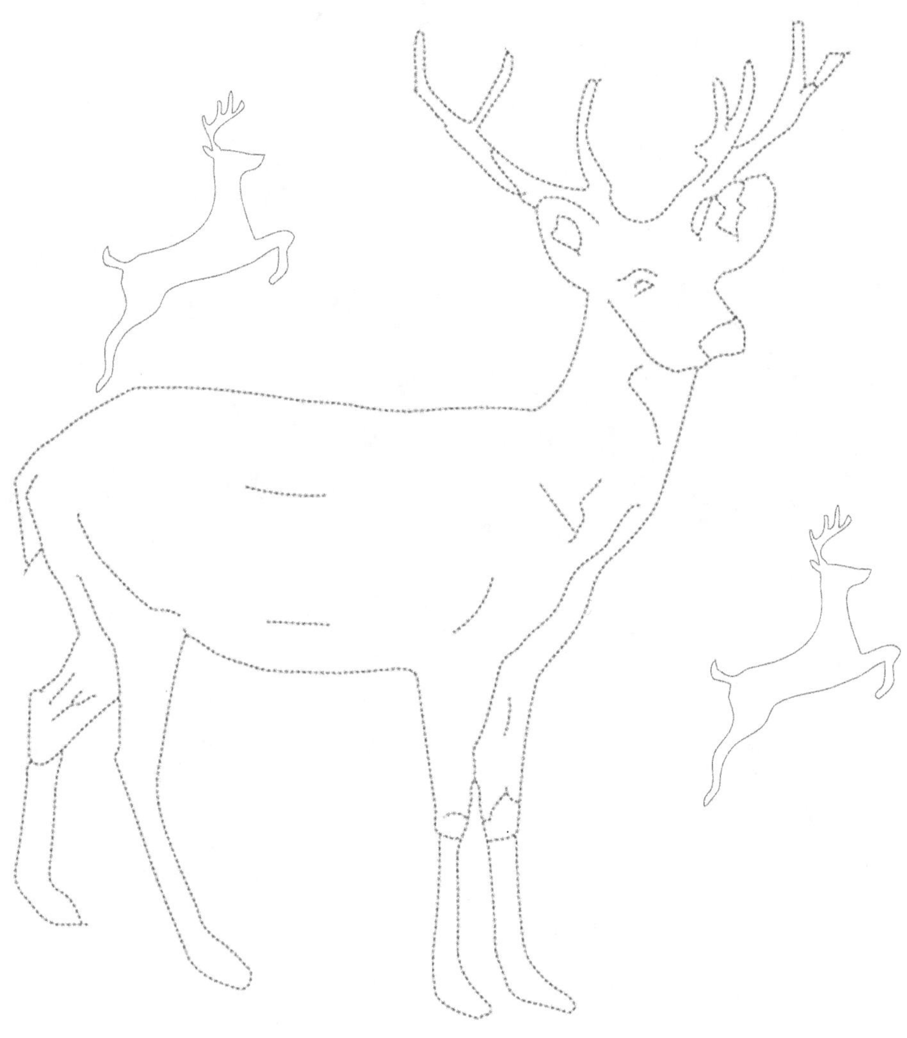

Deer

TRYING AREA

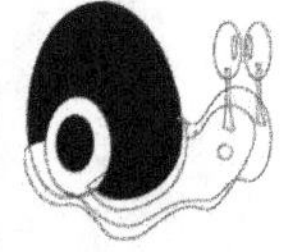

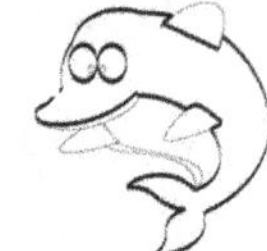

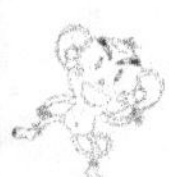
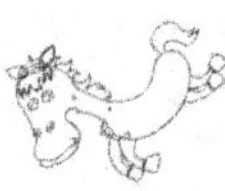
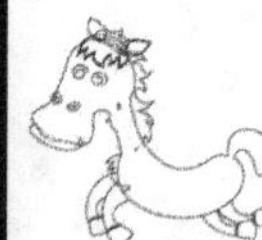

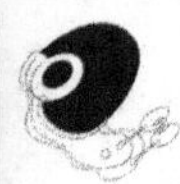
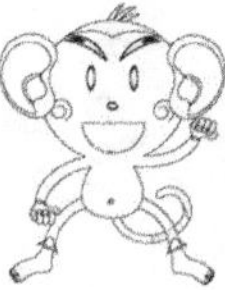
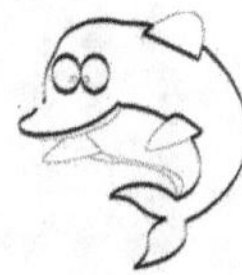
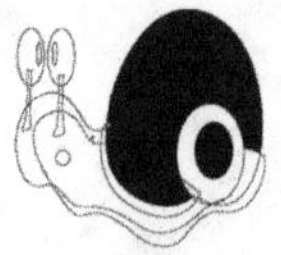

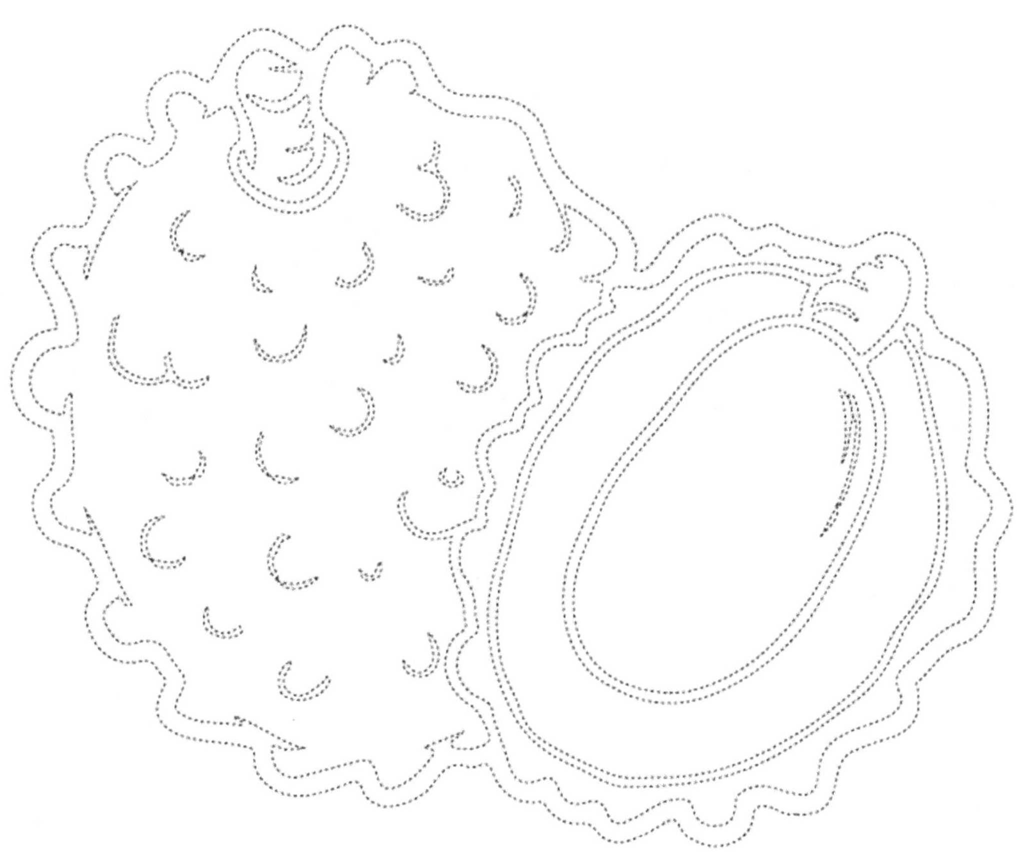

Lychee

TRYING AREA

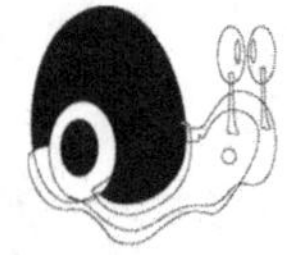

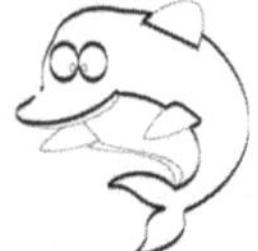

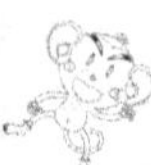
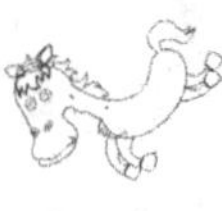
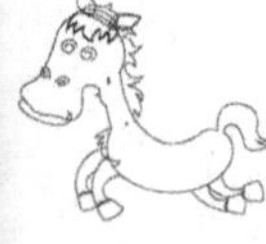

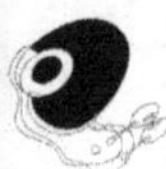
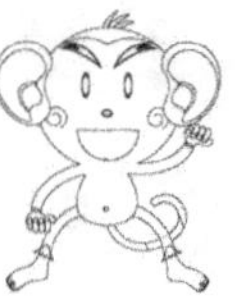
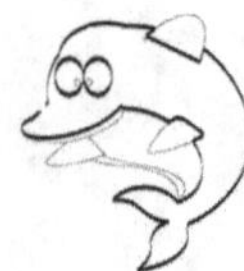
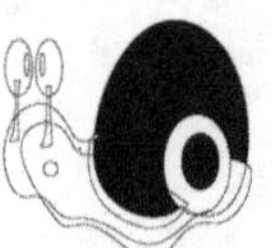

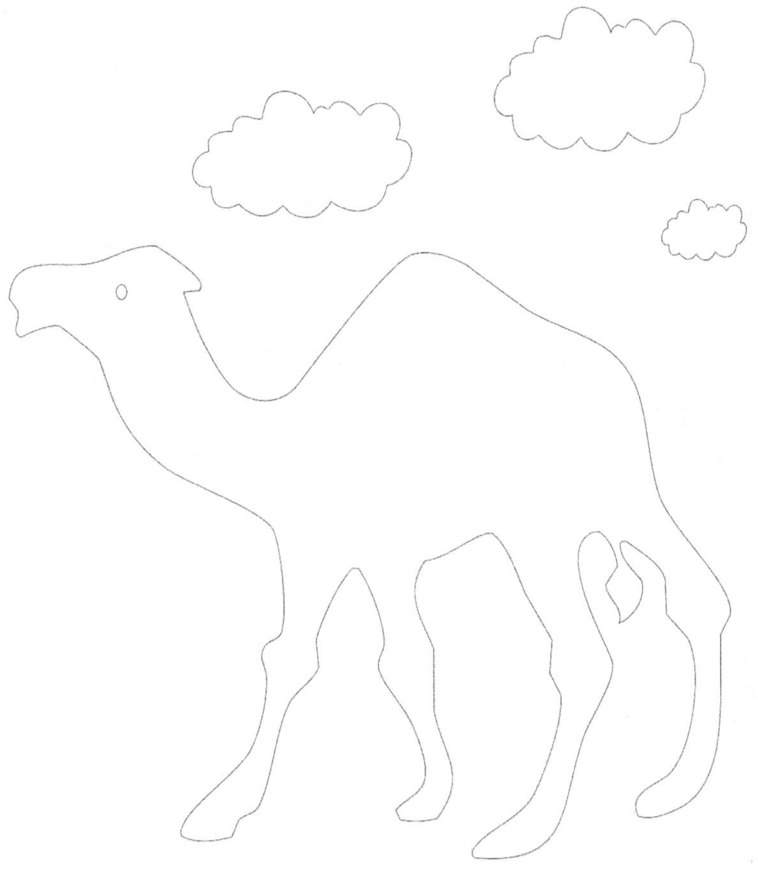

Kamel

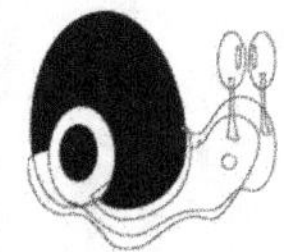

TRYING AREA

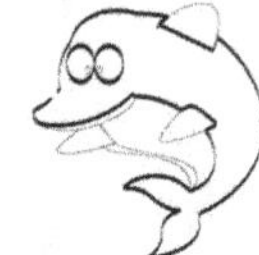

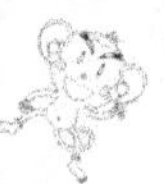
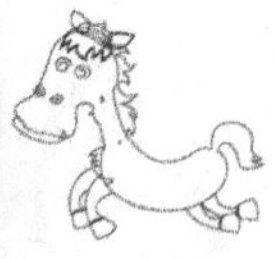
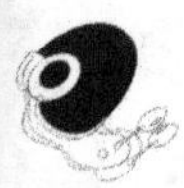
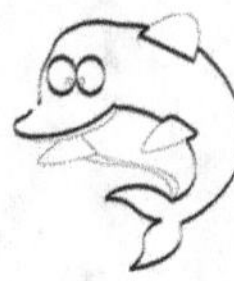
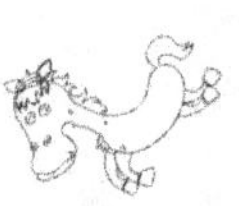

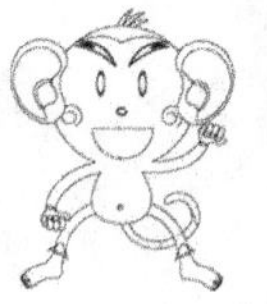
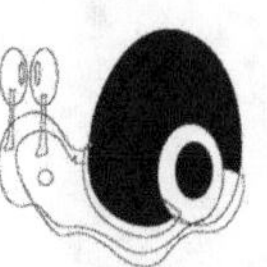

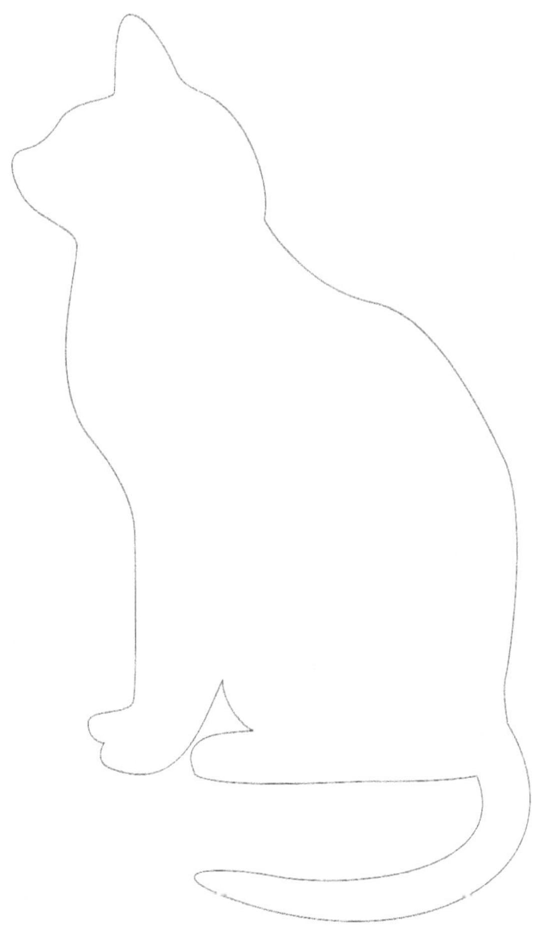

Cat

TRYING AREA

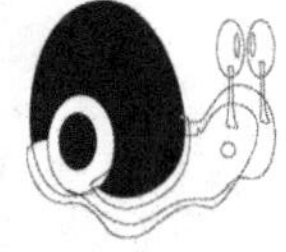

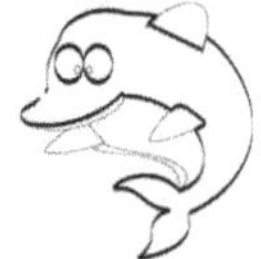

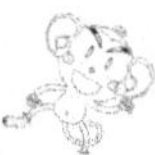
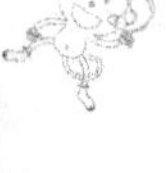
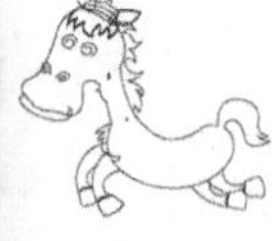
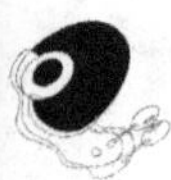
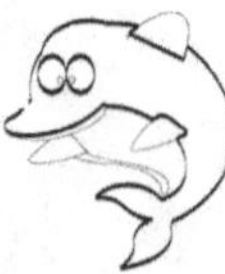
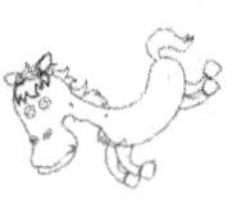

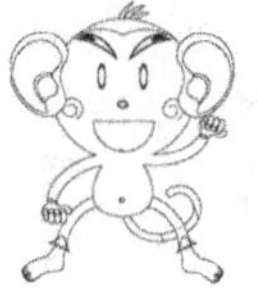
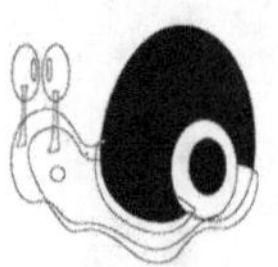

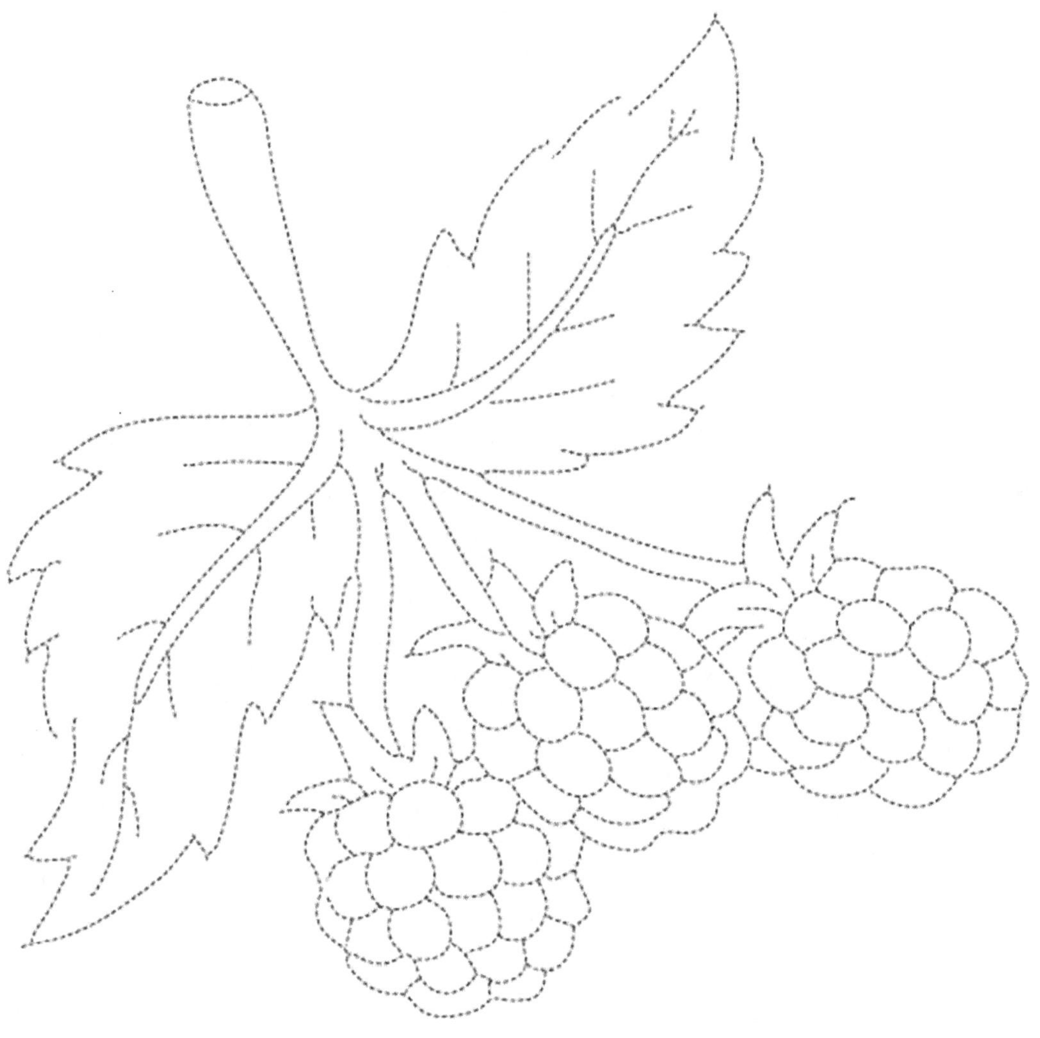

raspberries

TRYING AREA

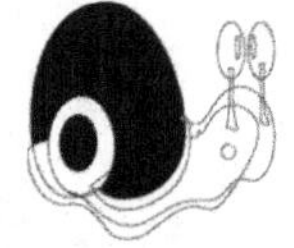

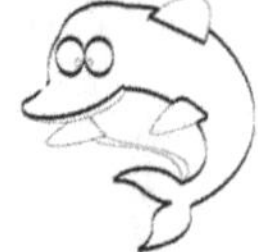

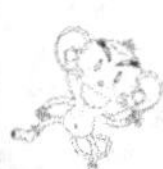
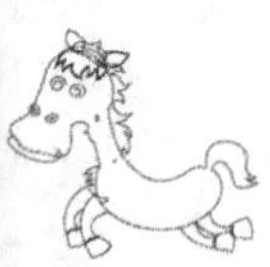
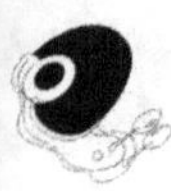
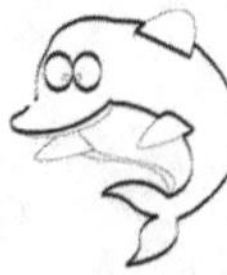
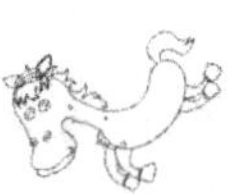

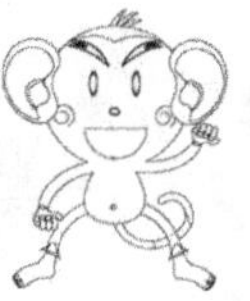
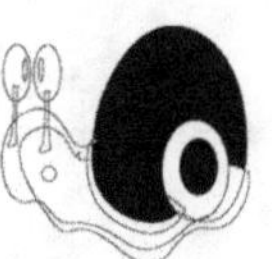

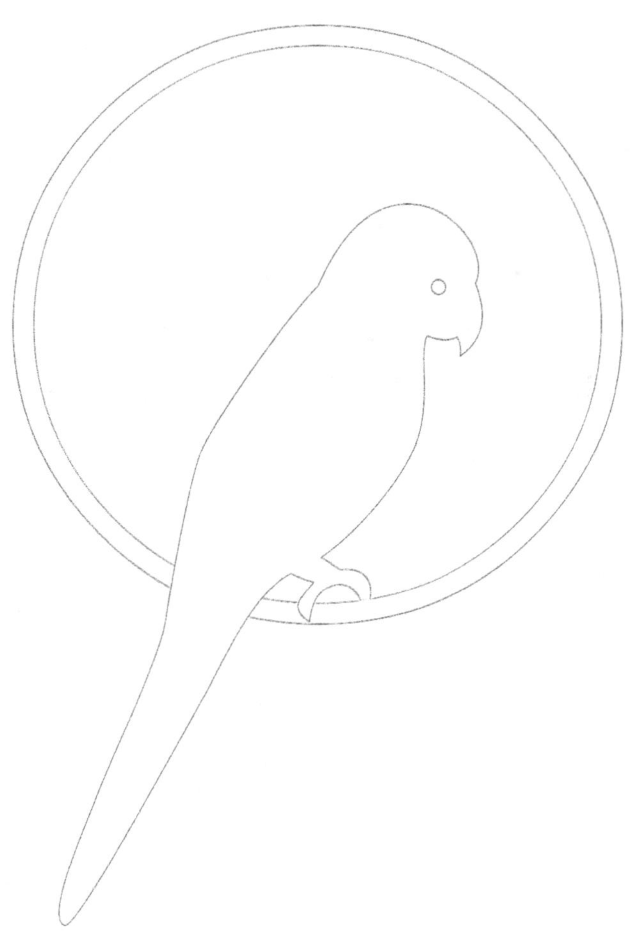

Bird

TRYING AREA

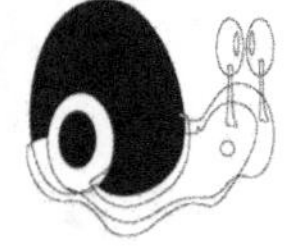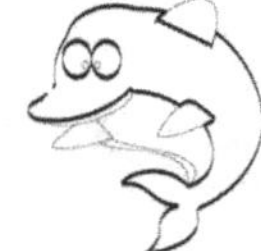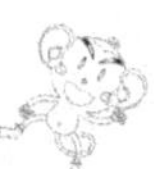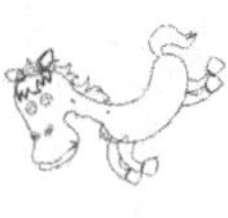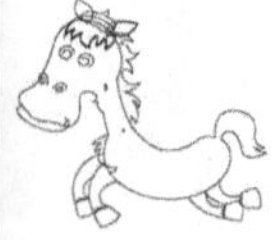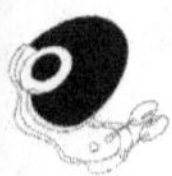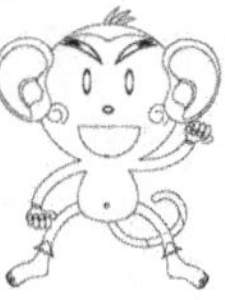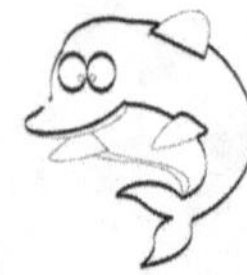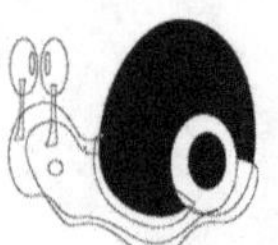

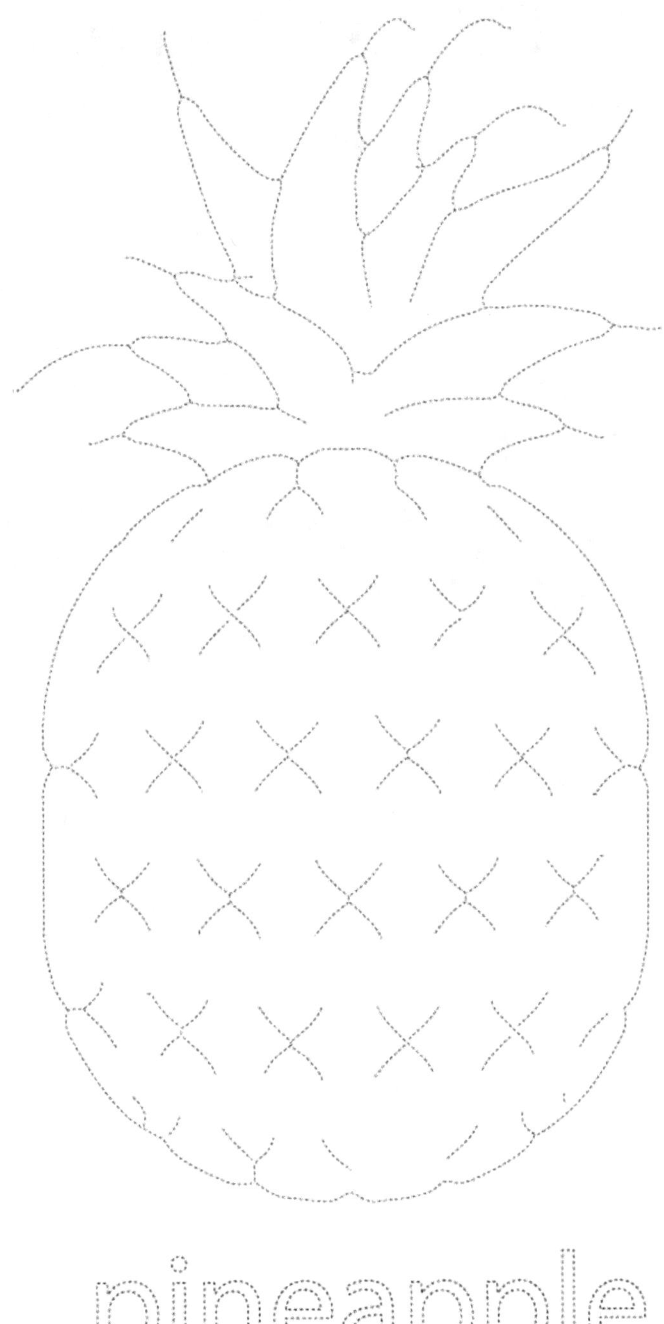

pineapple

TRYING AREA

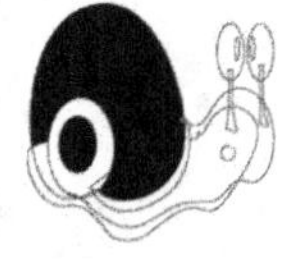

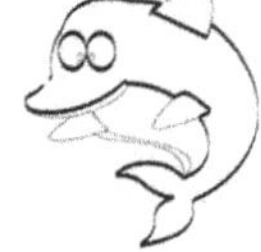

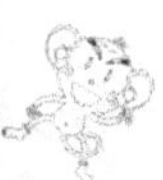
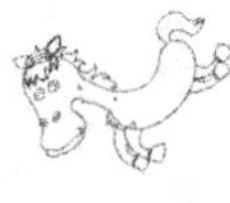
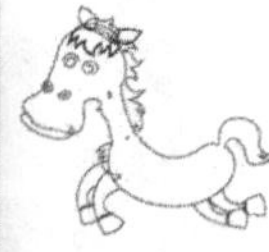

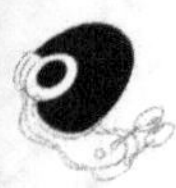
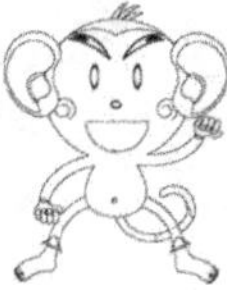
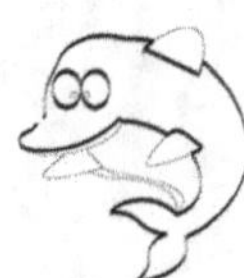
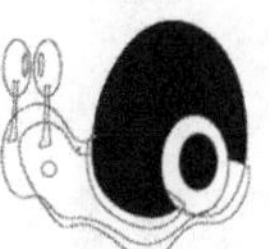

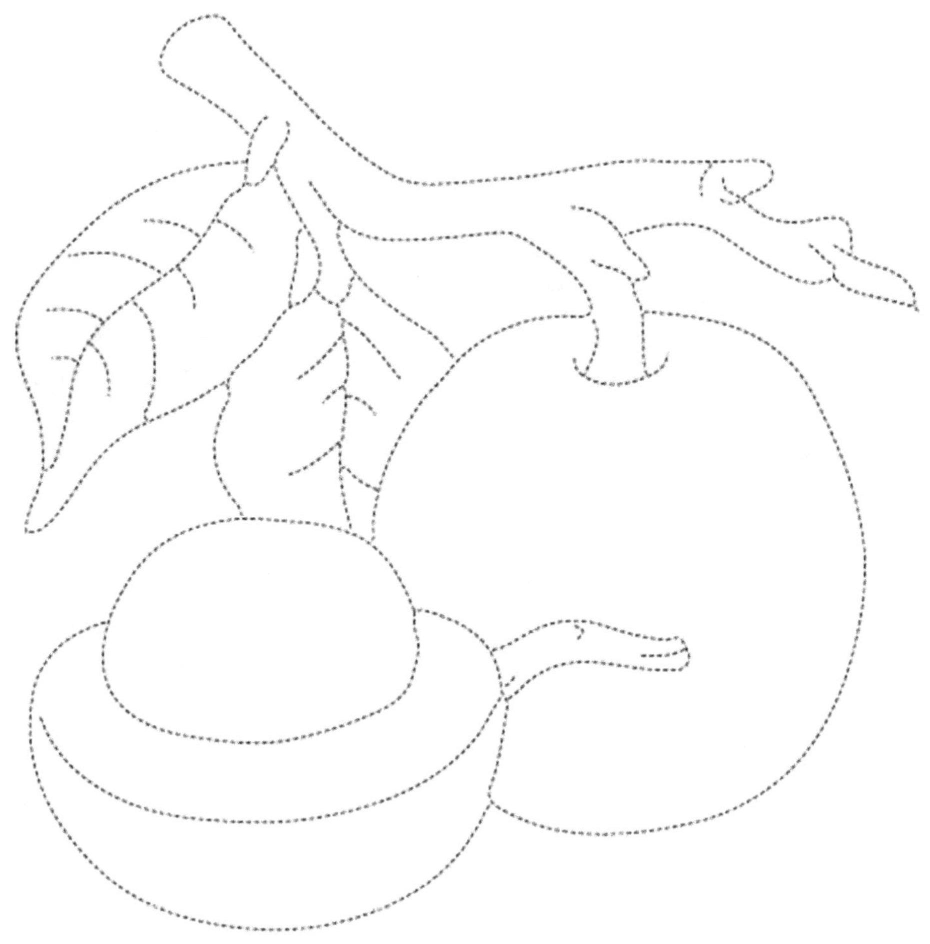

Tallow-wood

TRYING AREA

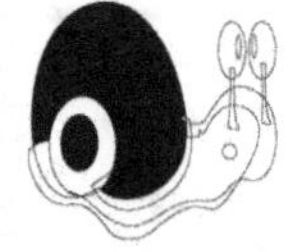

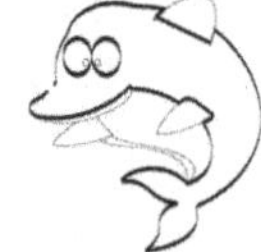

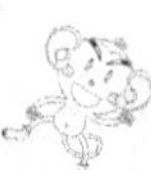
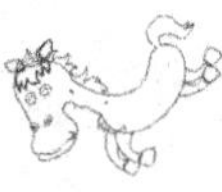
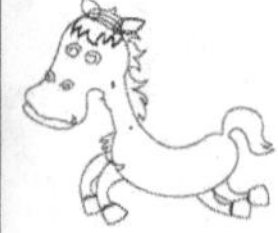

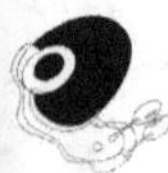
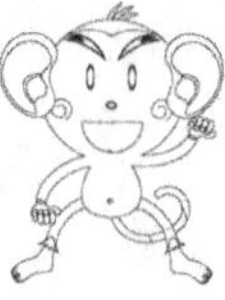
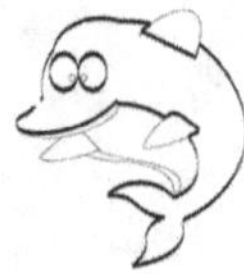
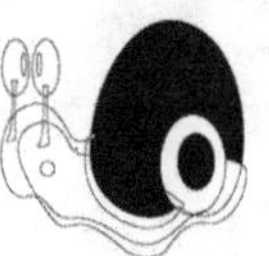

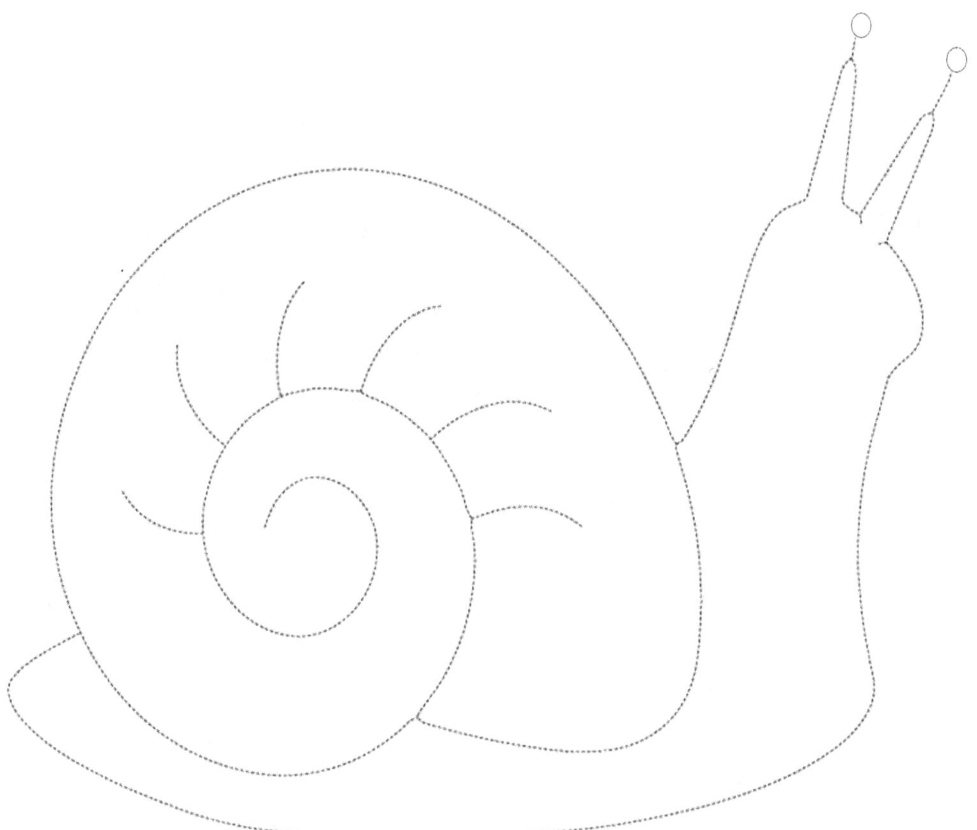

Snail

TRYING AREA

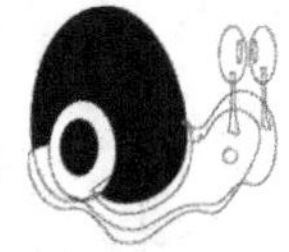

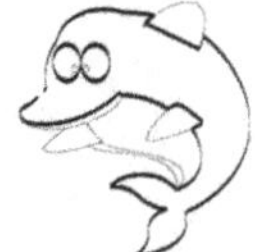

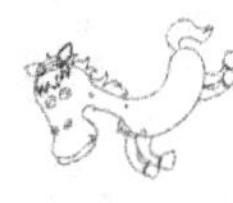
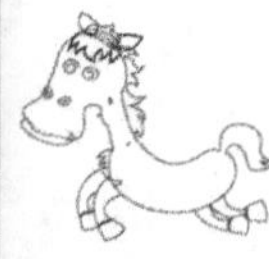

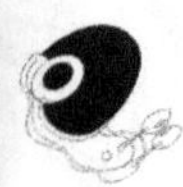
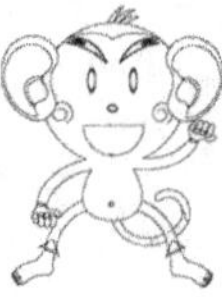
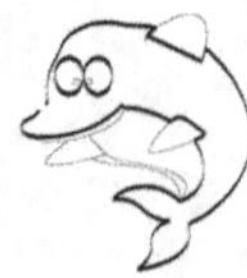
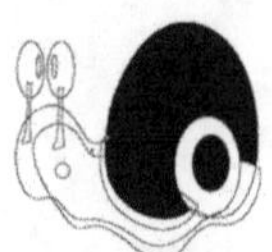

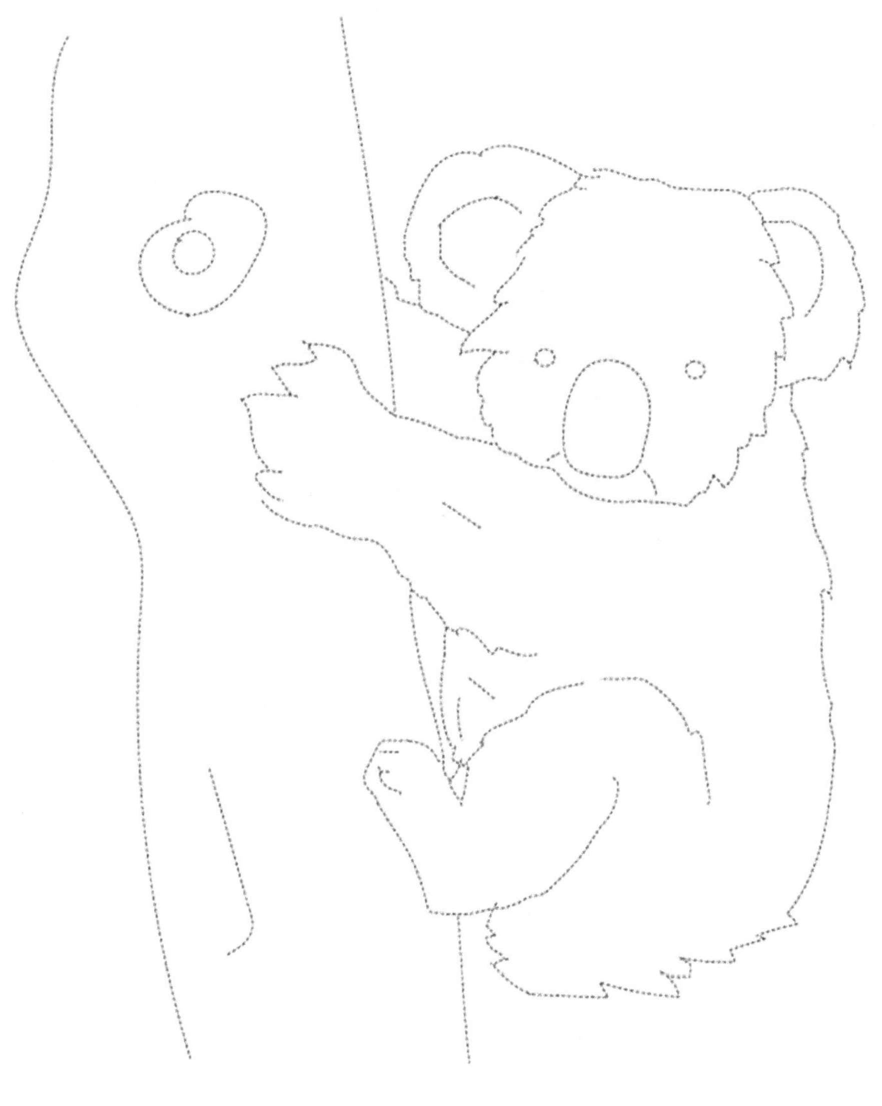

Koala

TRYING AREA

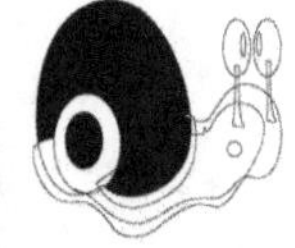

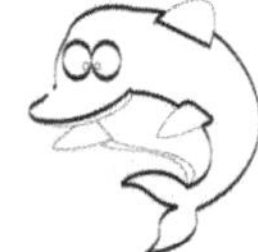

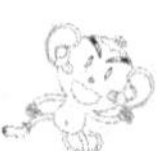
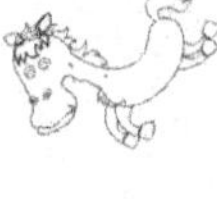
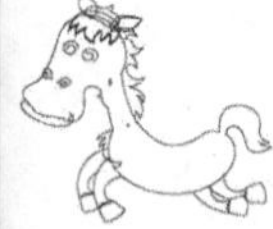

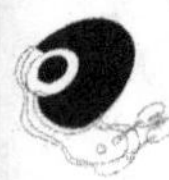
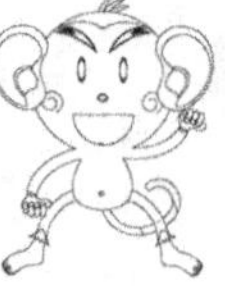
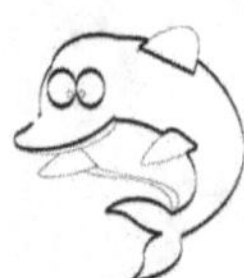
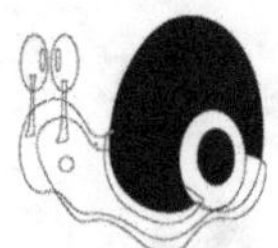

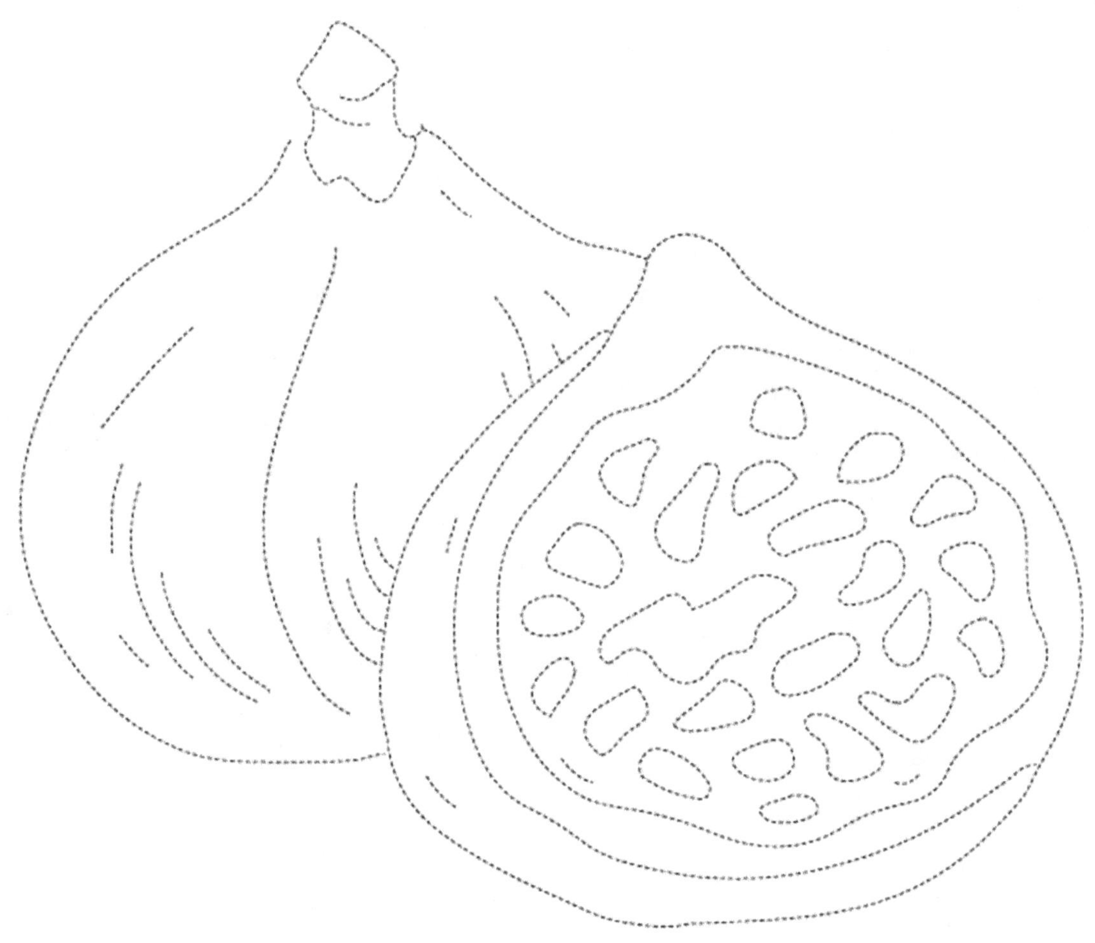

figs

TRYING AREA

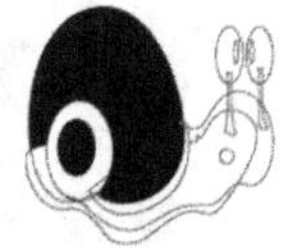

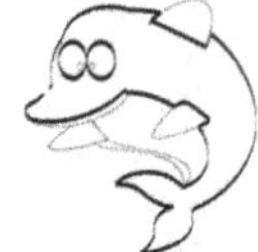

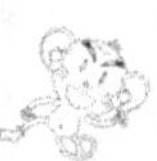
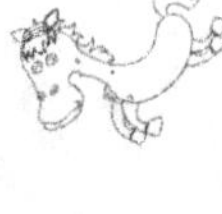

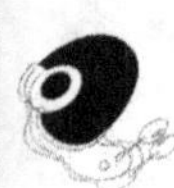
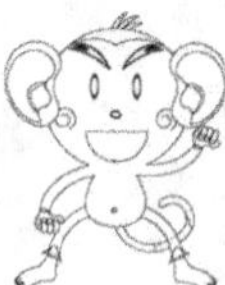
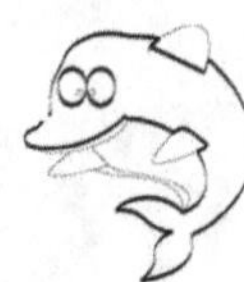
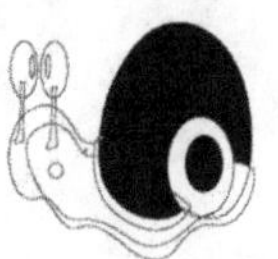

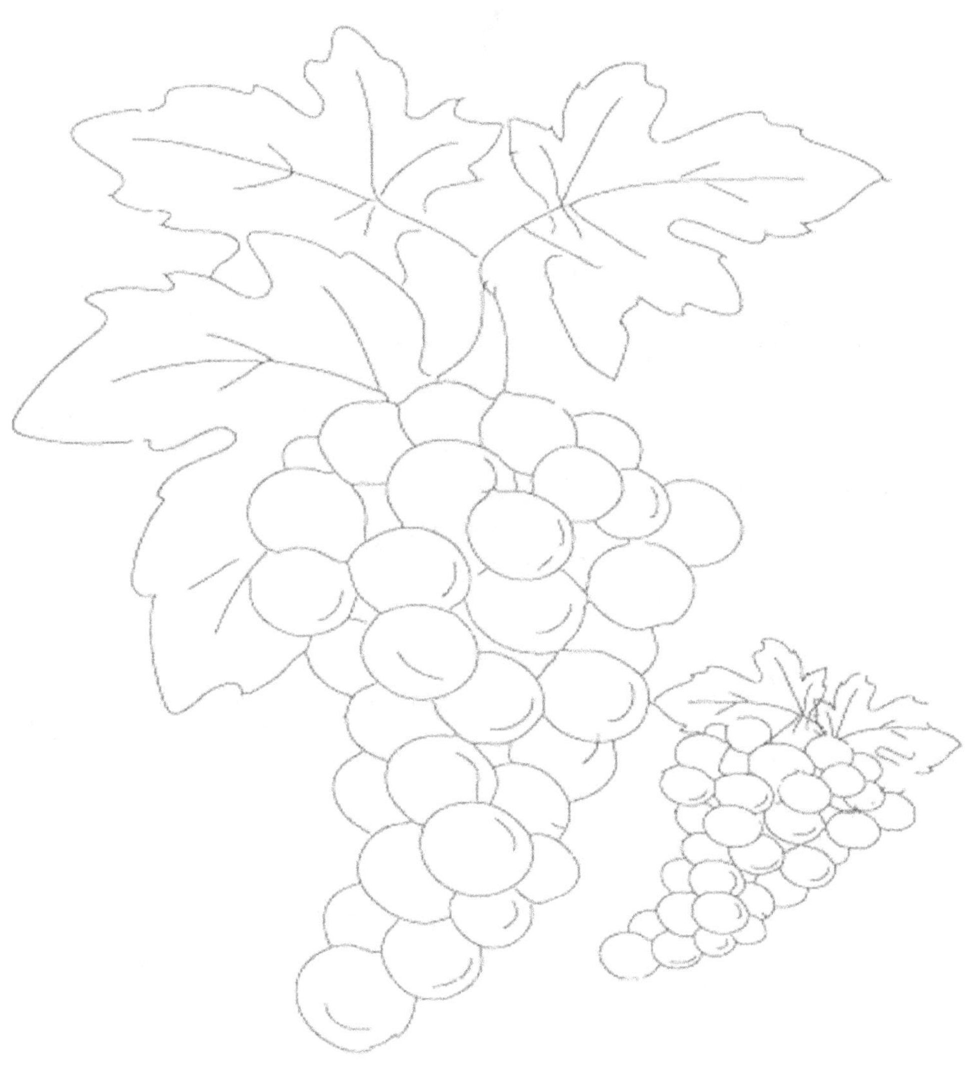

grapes

TRYING AREA

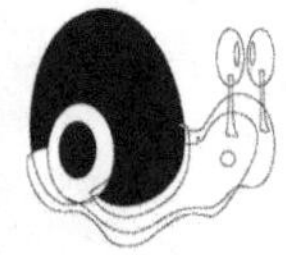

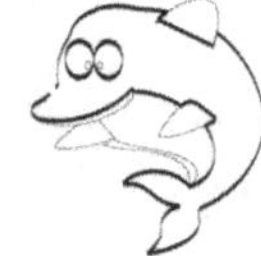

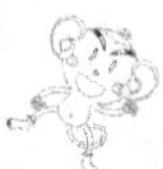
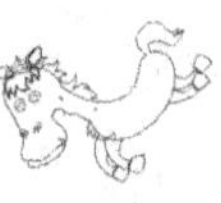

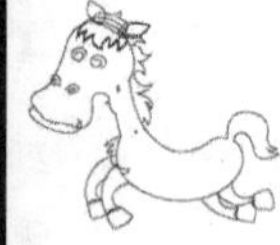
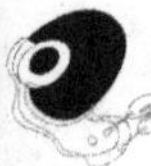
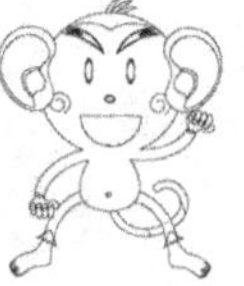
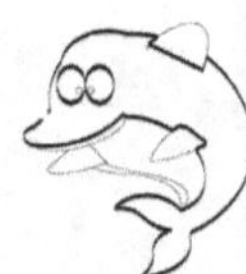
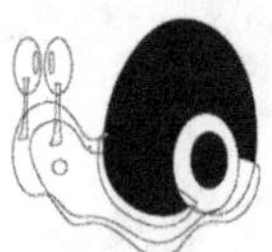

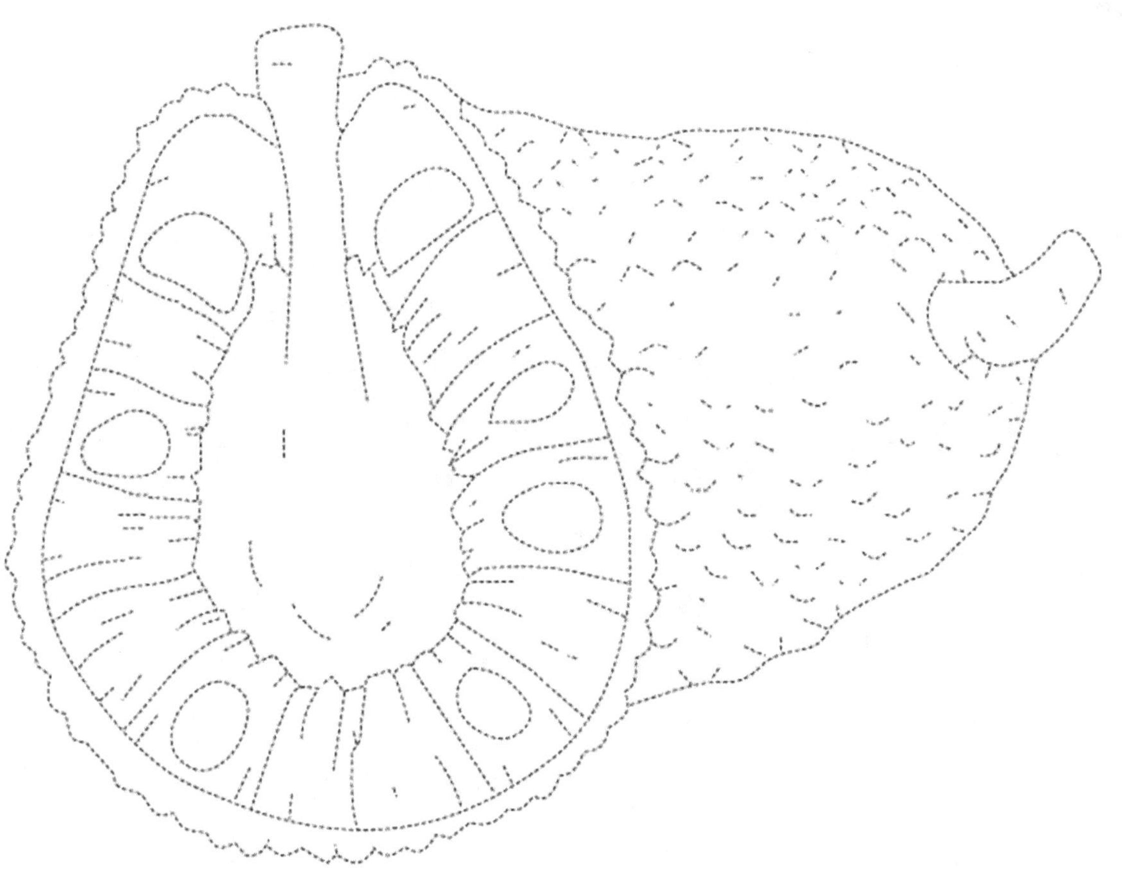

Yaca

TRYING AREA

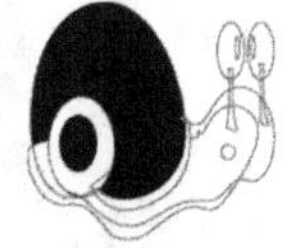

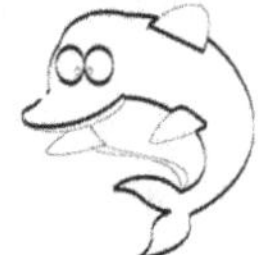

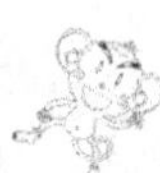
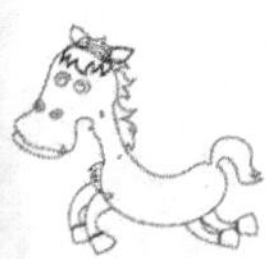
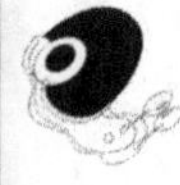
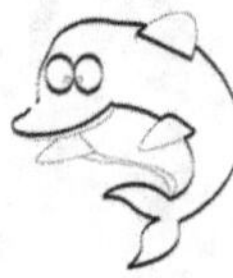
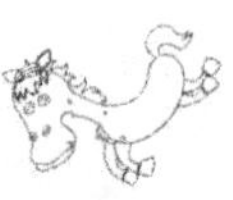

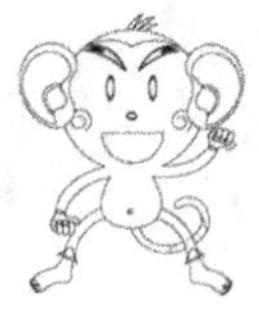
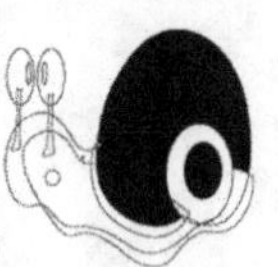

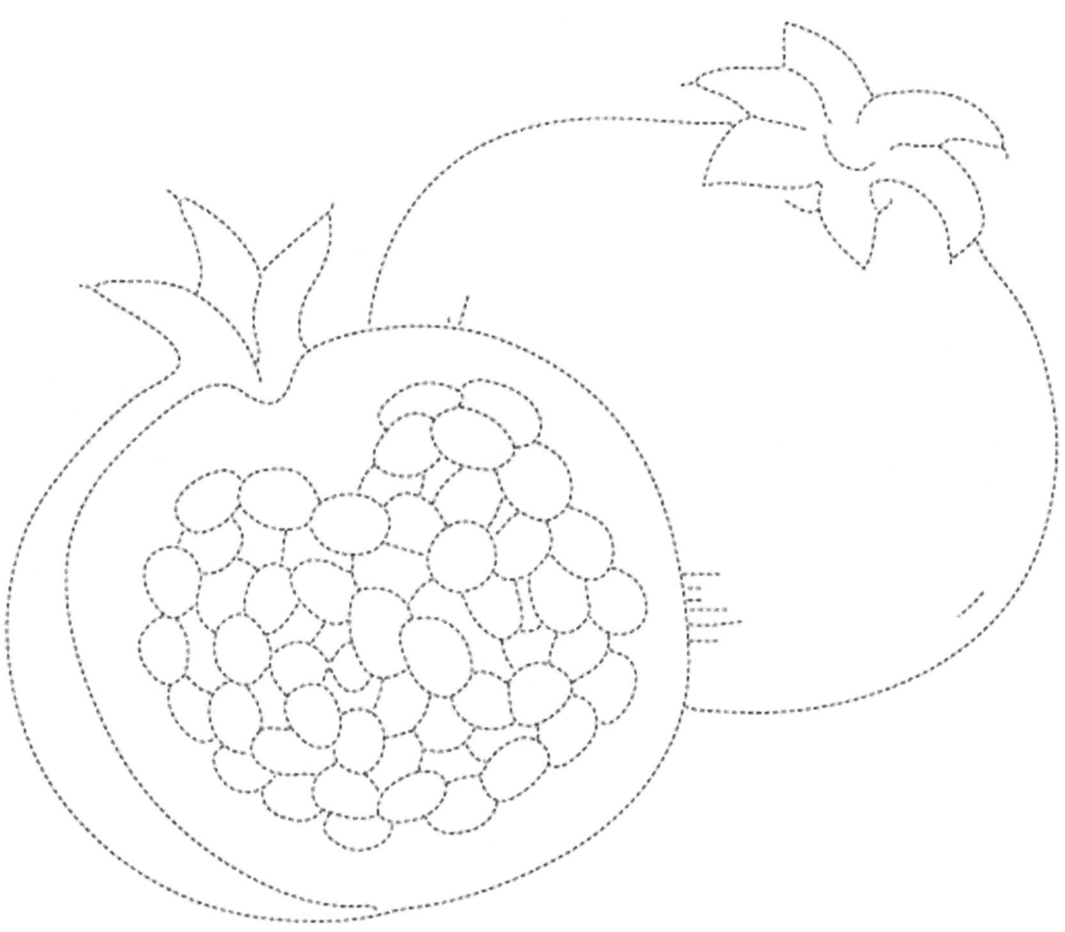

pomegranate

TRYING AREA

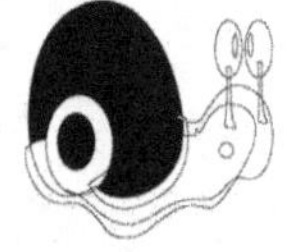

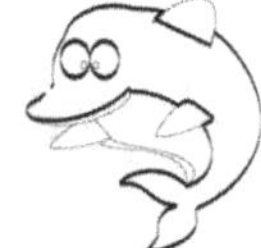

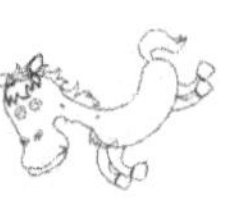
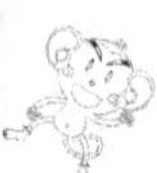

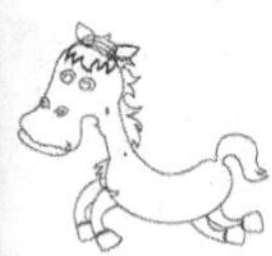
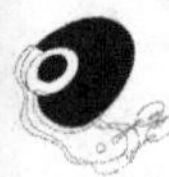
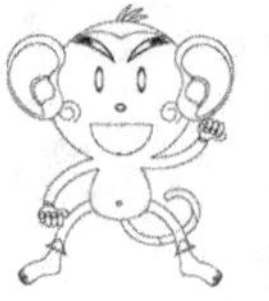
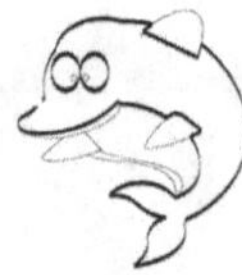
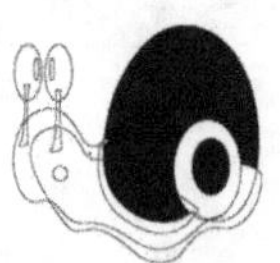

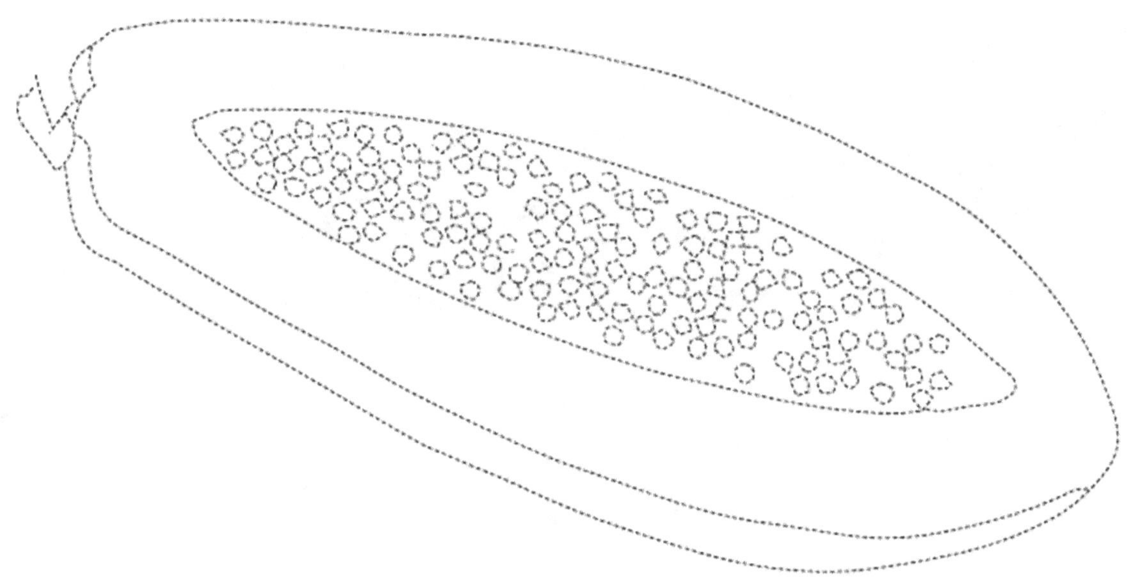

papaya

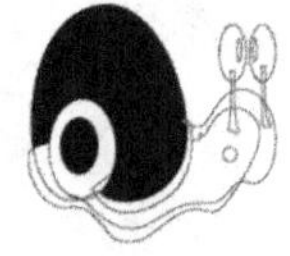

TRYING AREA

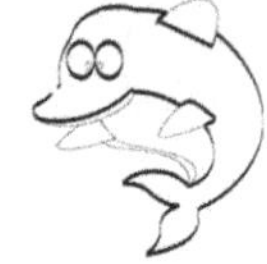

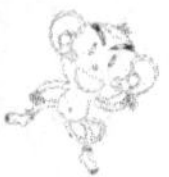
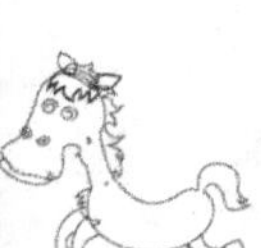
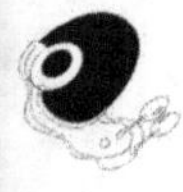
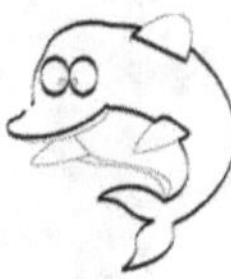
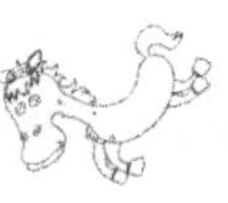

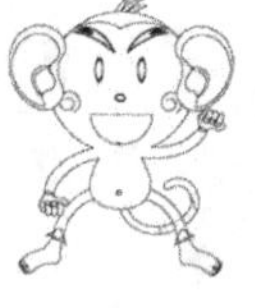
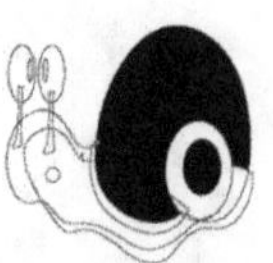

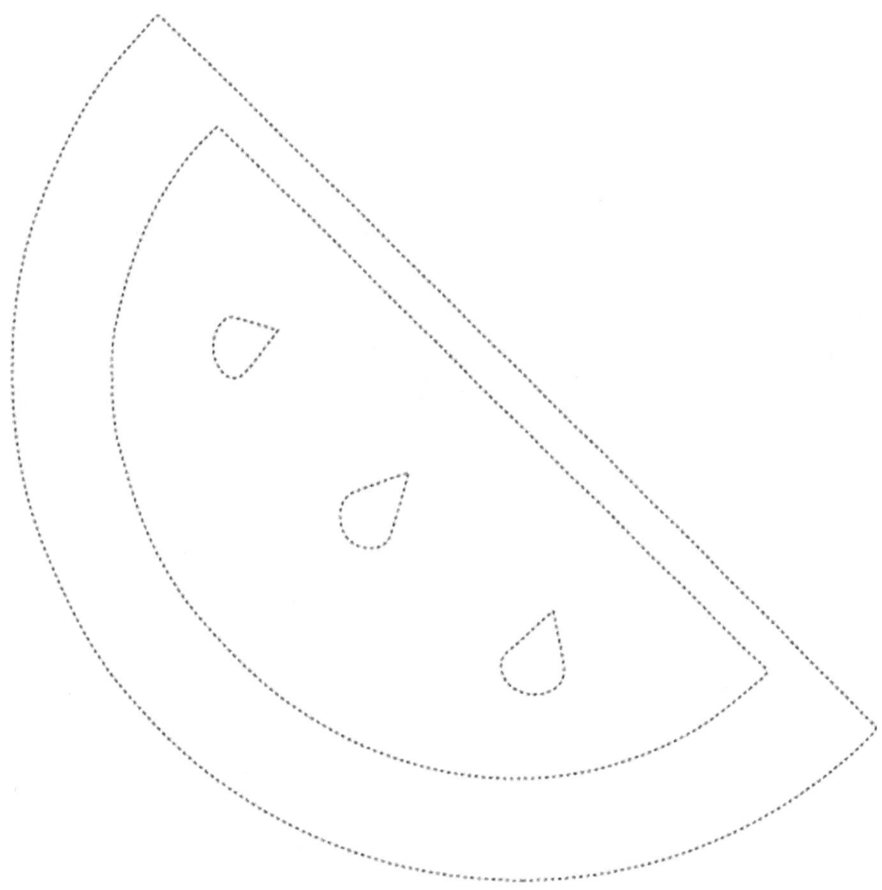

watermelon

TRYING AREA

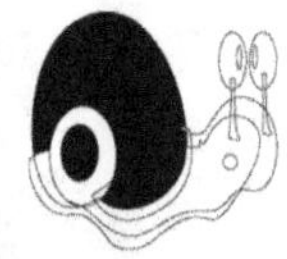

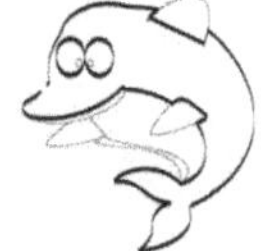

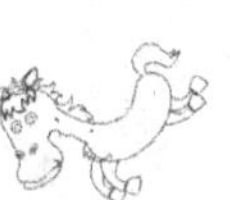
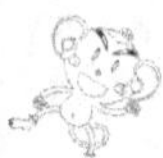

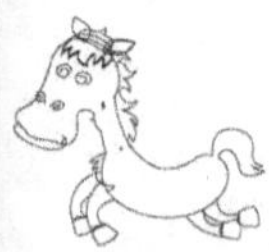
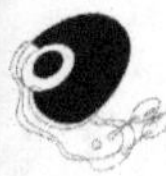
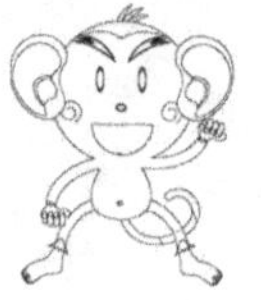
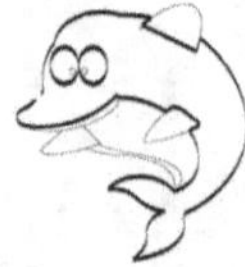
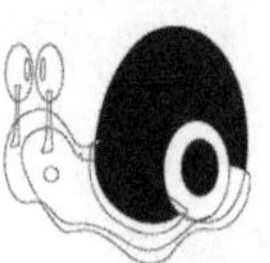

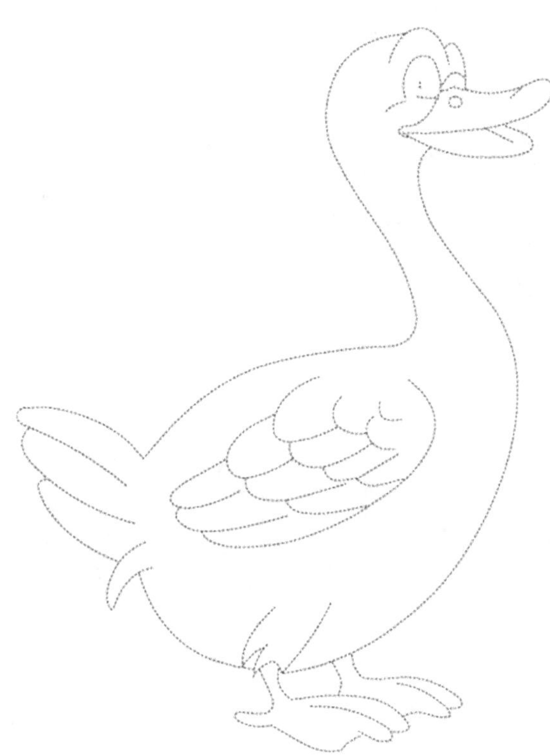

d u c k

TRYING AREA

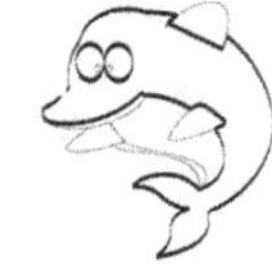

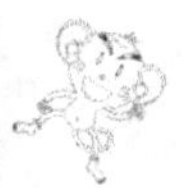
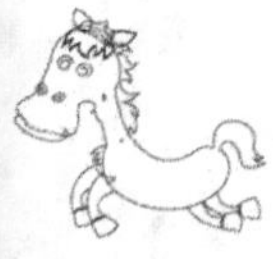
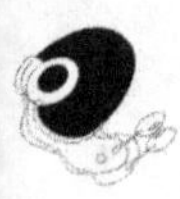
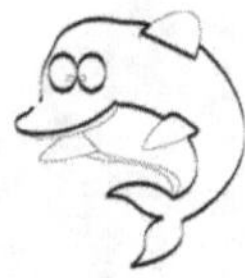
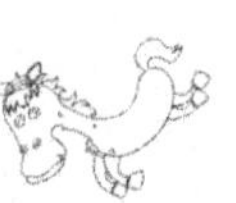

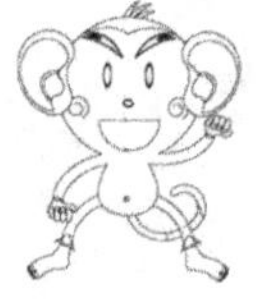
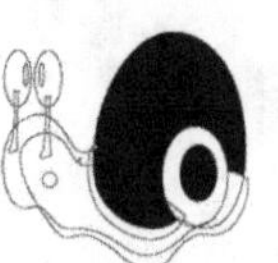

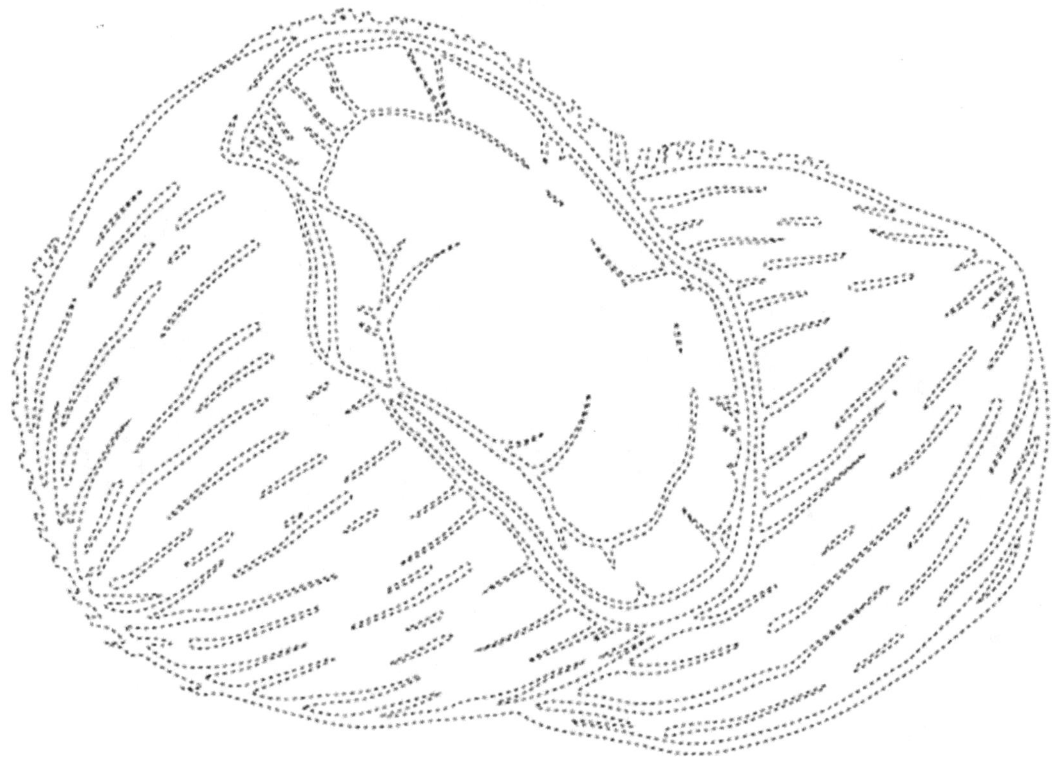

coconut

TRYING AREA

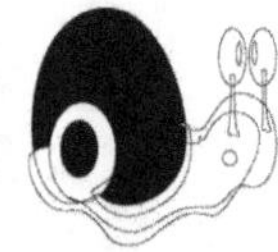

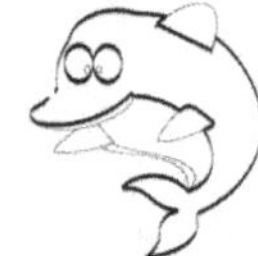

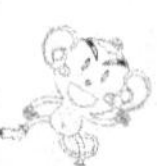
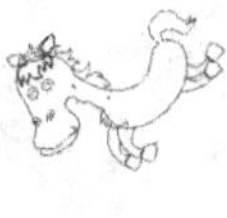
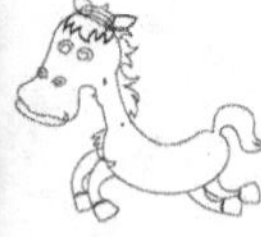

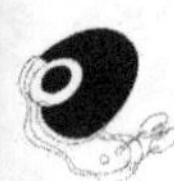
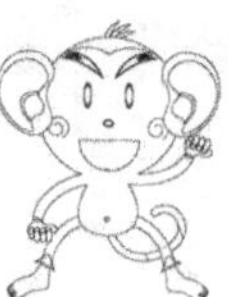
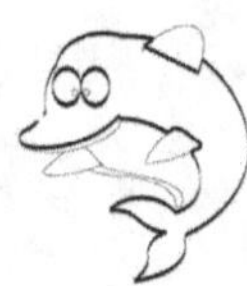
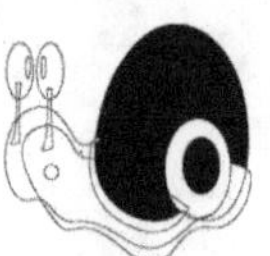

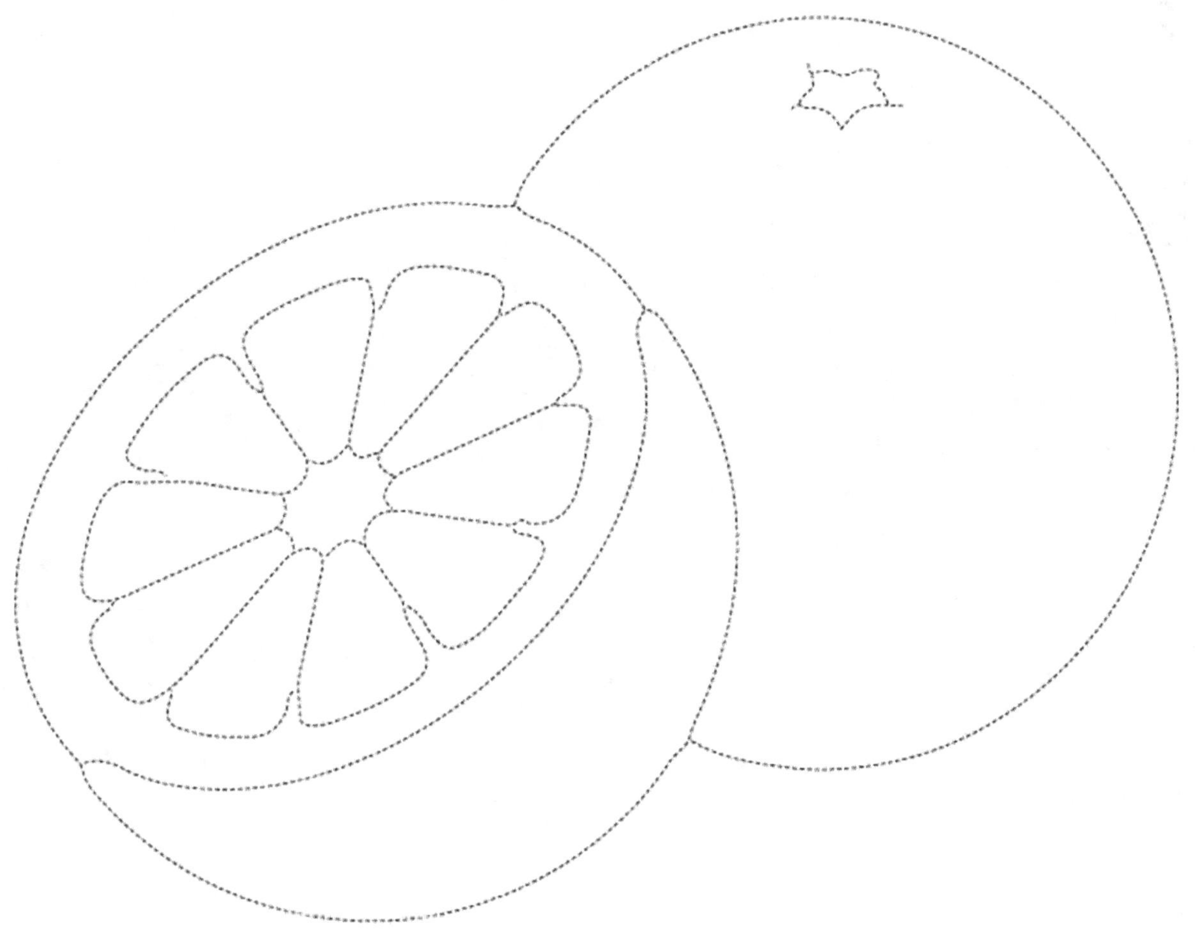

orange

TRYING AREA

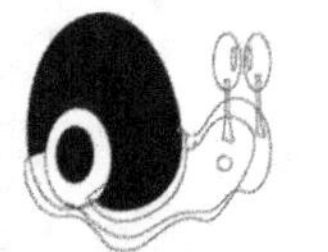

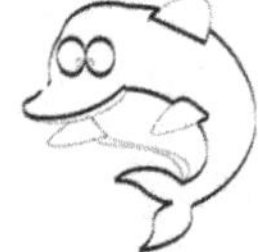

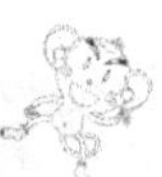
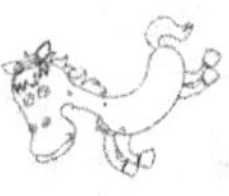
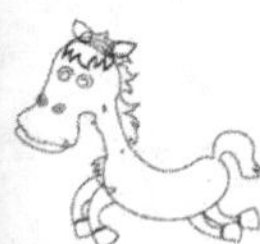

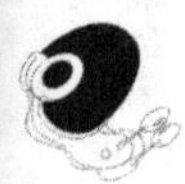
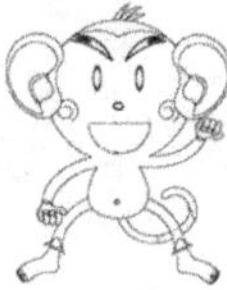
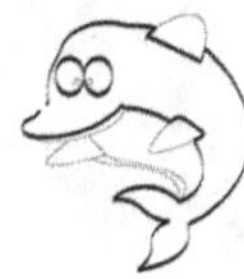
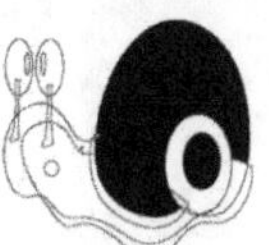

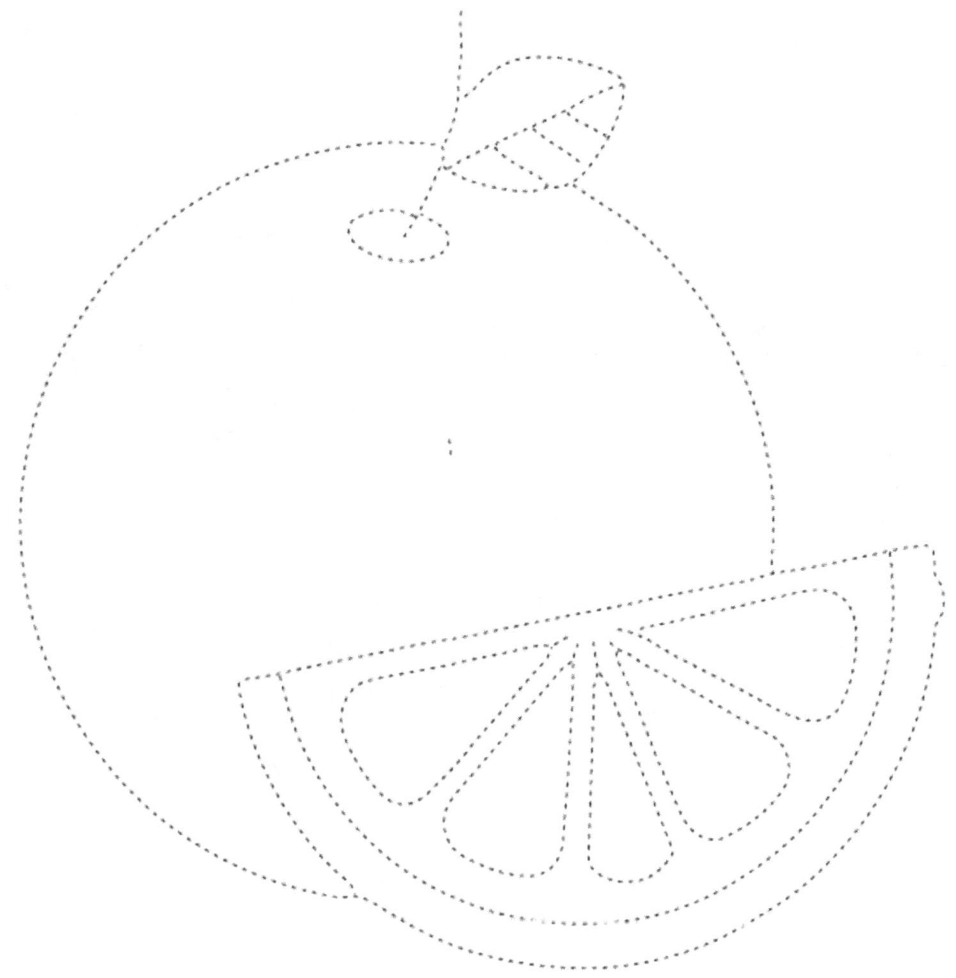

grapefruit

TRYING AREA

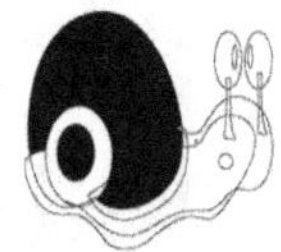

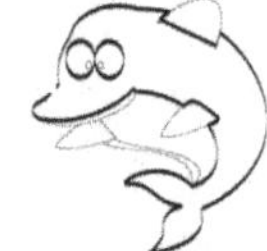

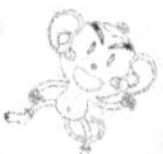
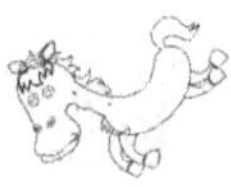

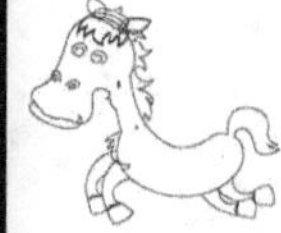
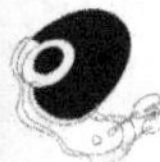
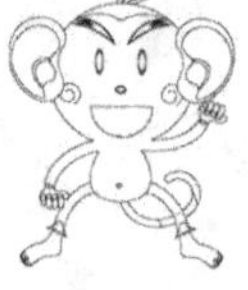
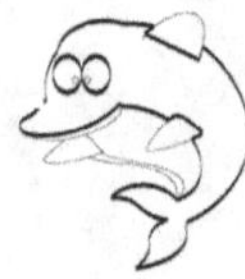
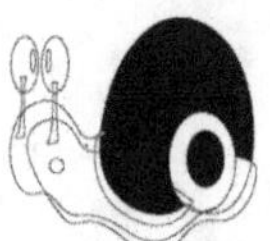

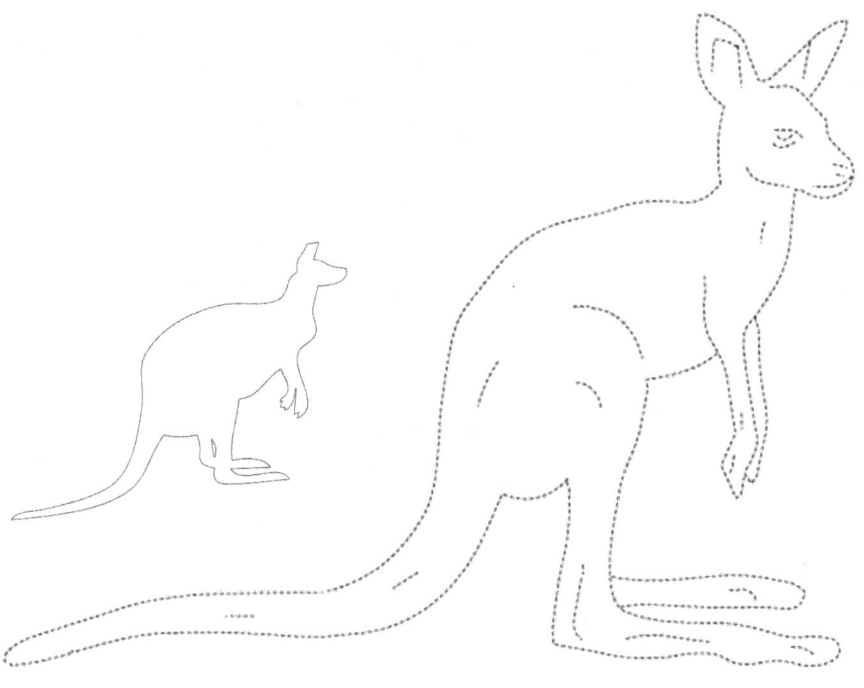

Kangaroo

TRYING AREA

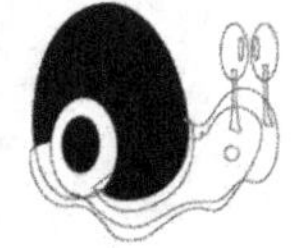

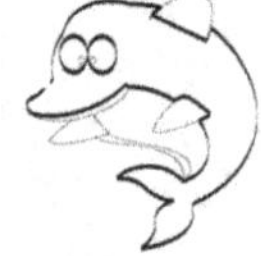

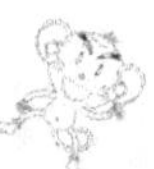
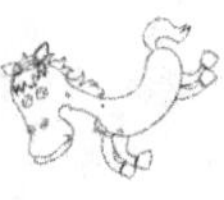
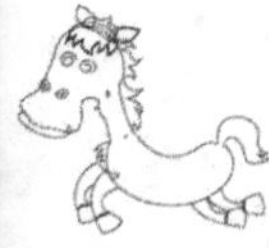

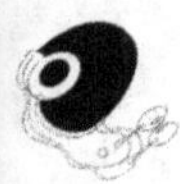
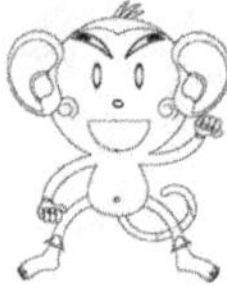
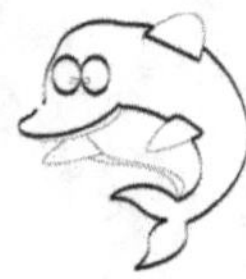
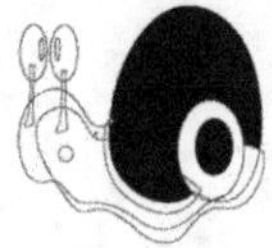

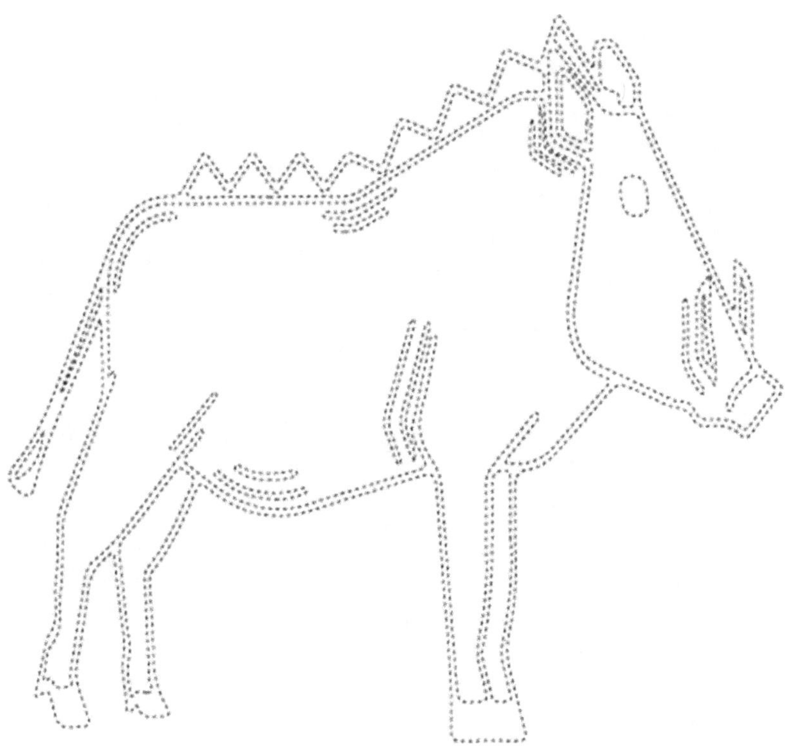

Pig

TRYING AREA

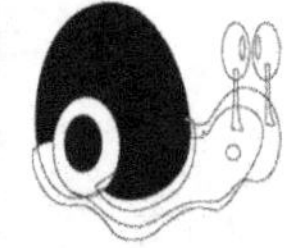

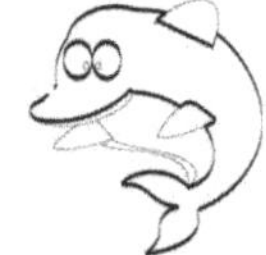

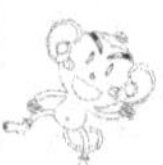
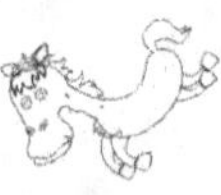

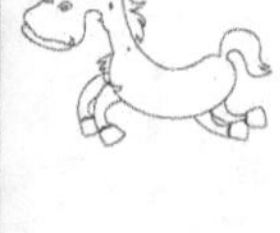
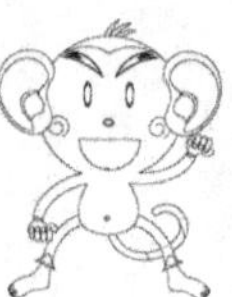
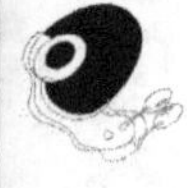
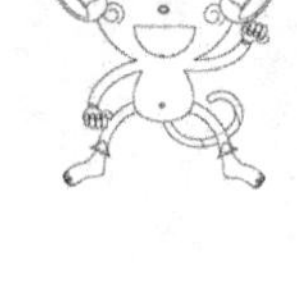
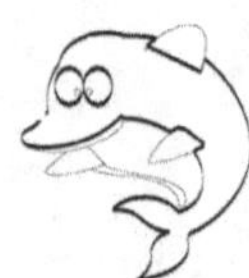
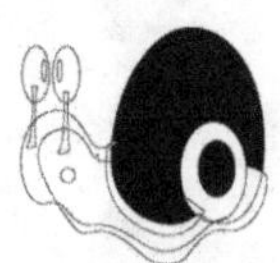

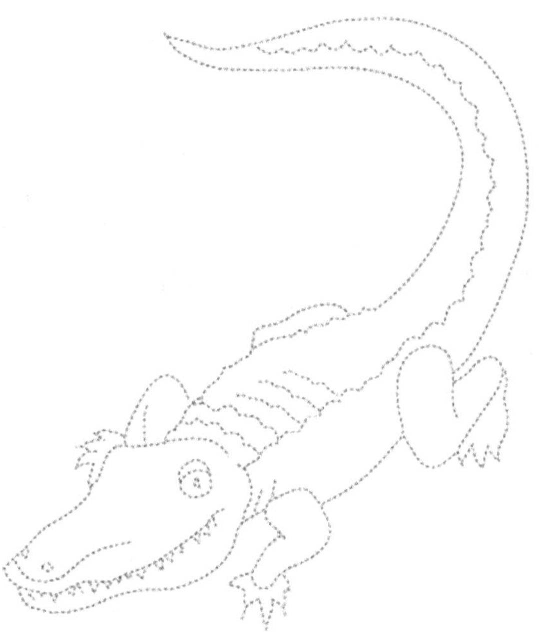

Alligator

TRYING AREA

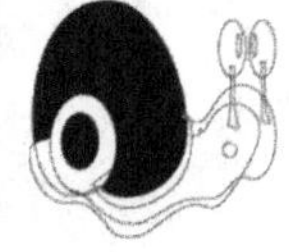

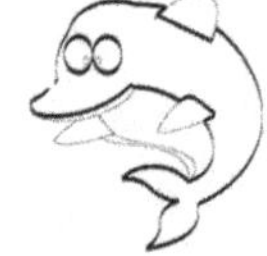

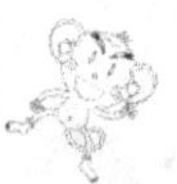
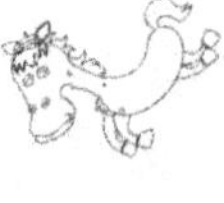
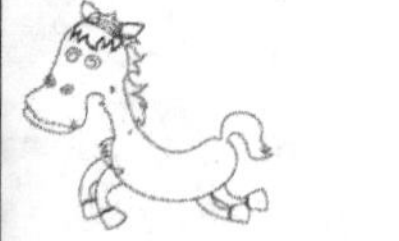

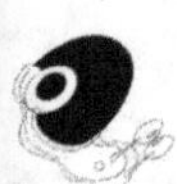
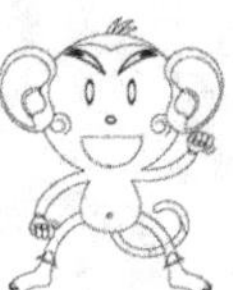
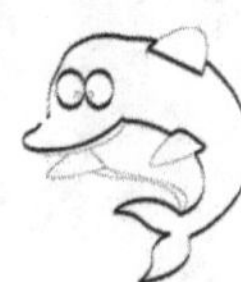
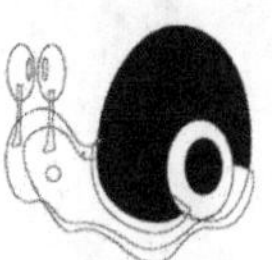

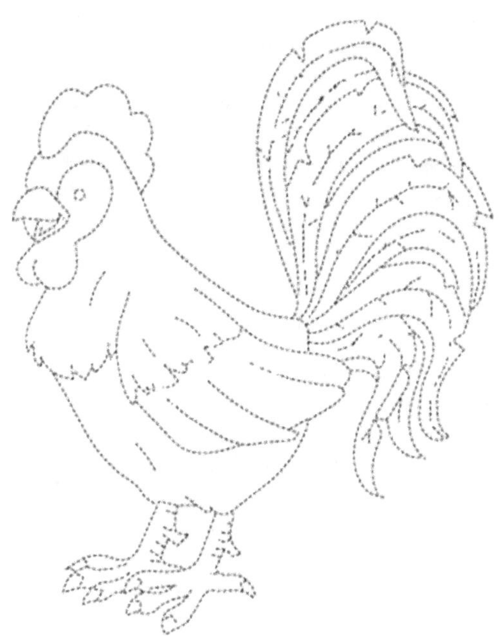

Chicken

TRYING AREA

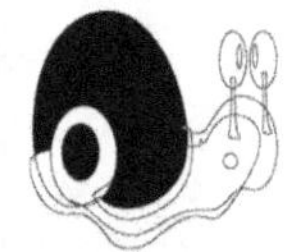

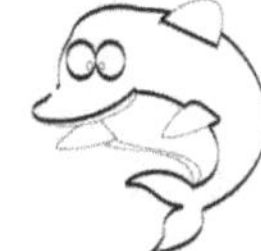

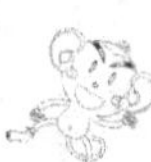
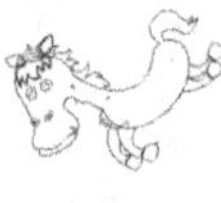
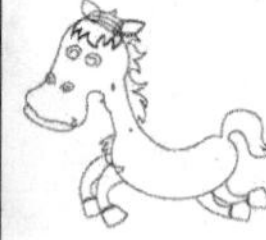

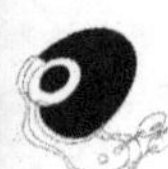
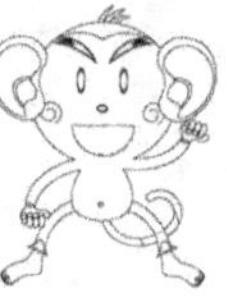
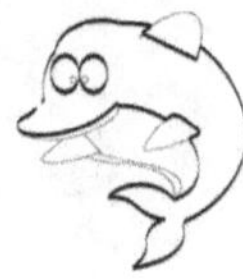
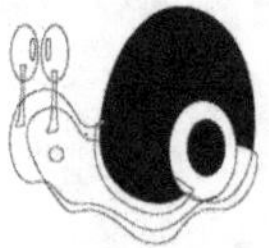

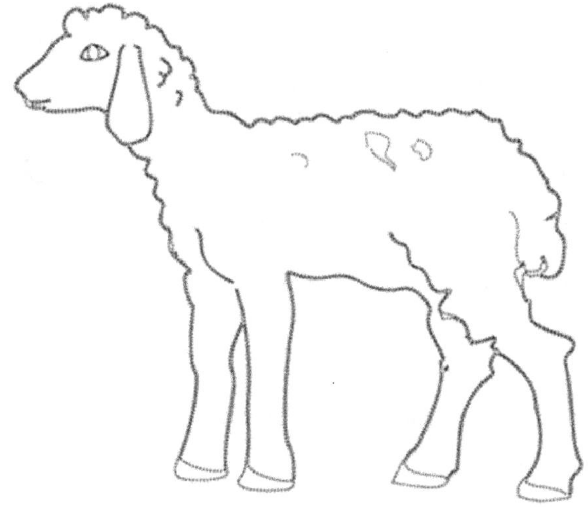

Lamb

TRYING AREA

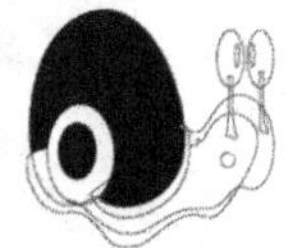

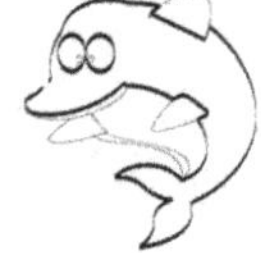

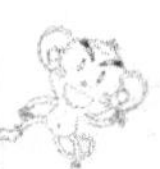
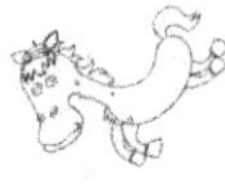
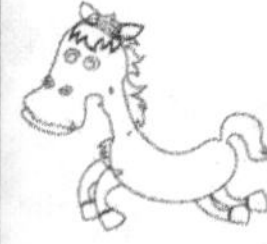

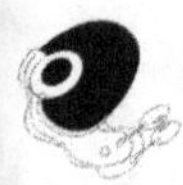
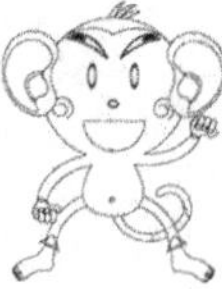
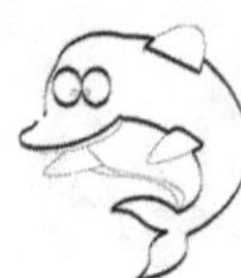
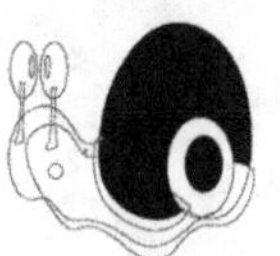

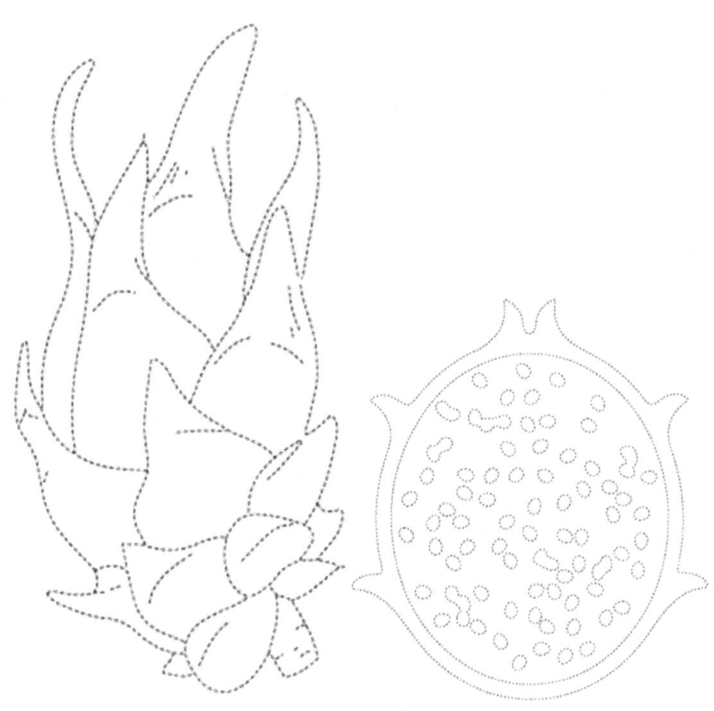

Dragon Fruit

TRYING AREA

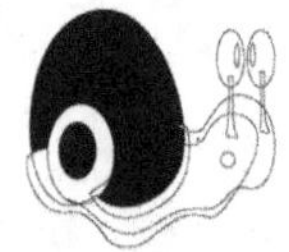

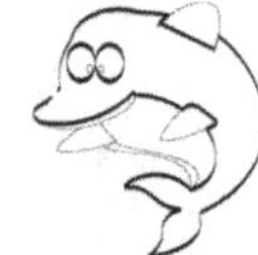

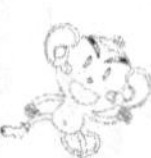
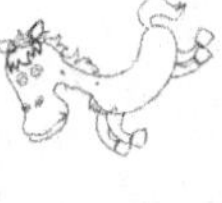

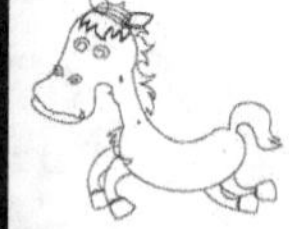
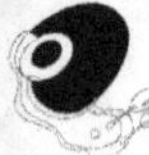
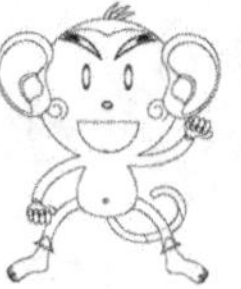
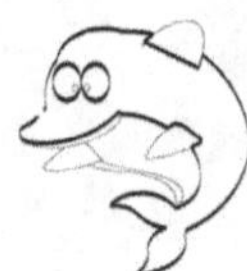
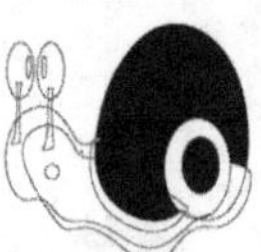

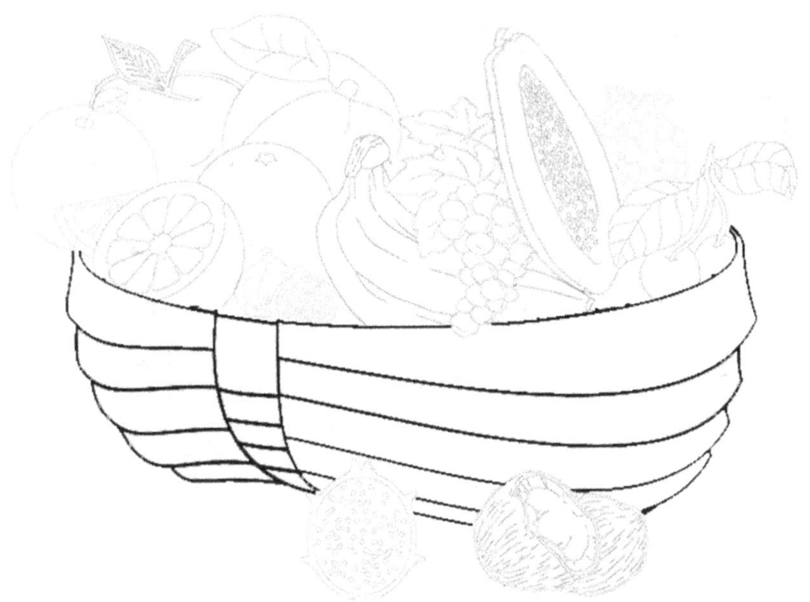

Basket Fruit

TRYING AREA

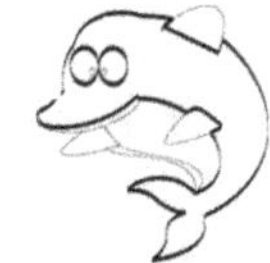

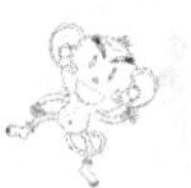
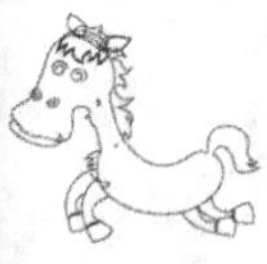
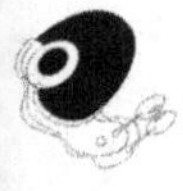
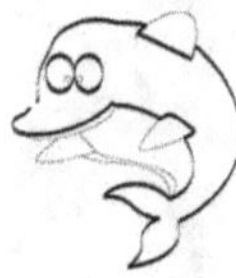
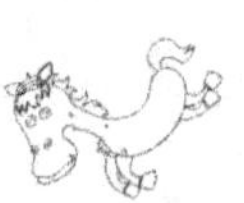

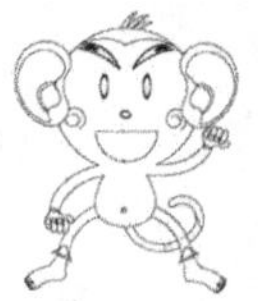
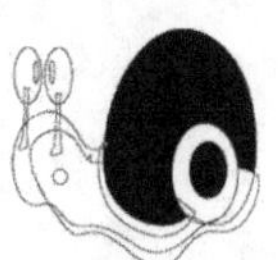

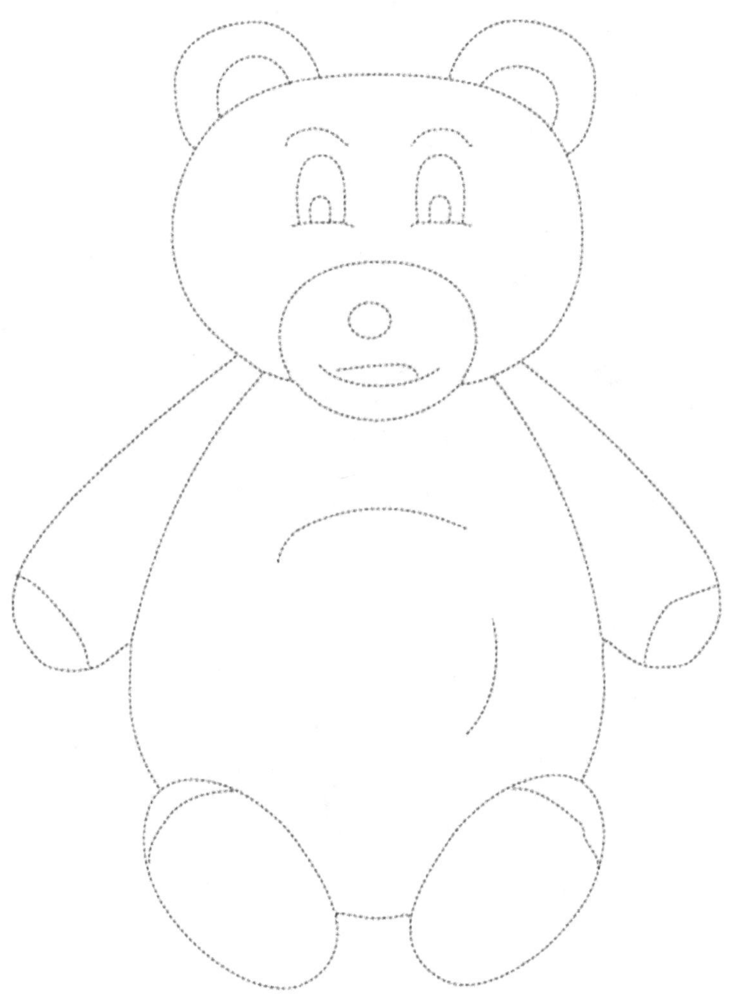

Bear

TRYING AREA

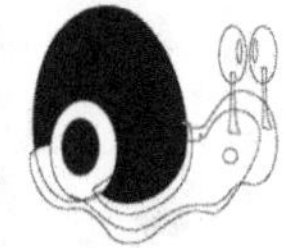

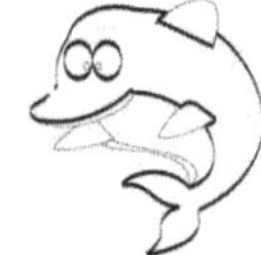

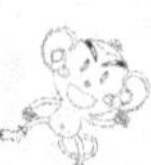
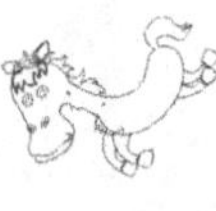
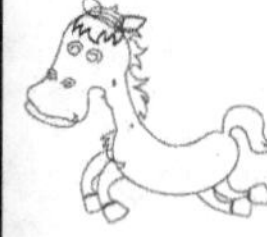

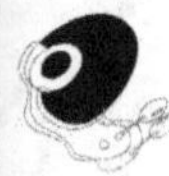
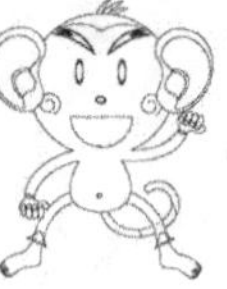
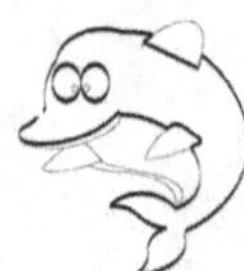
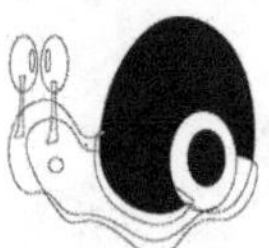

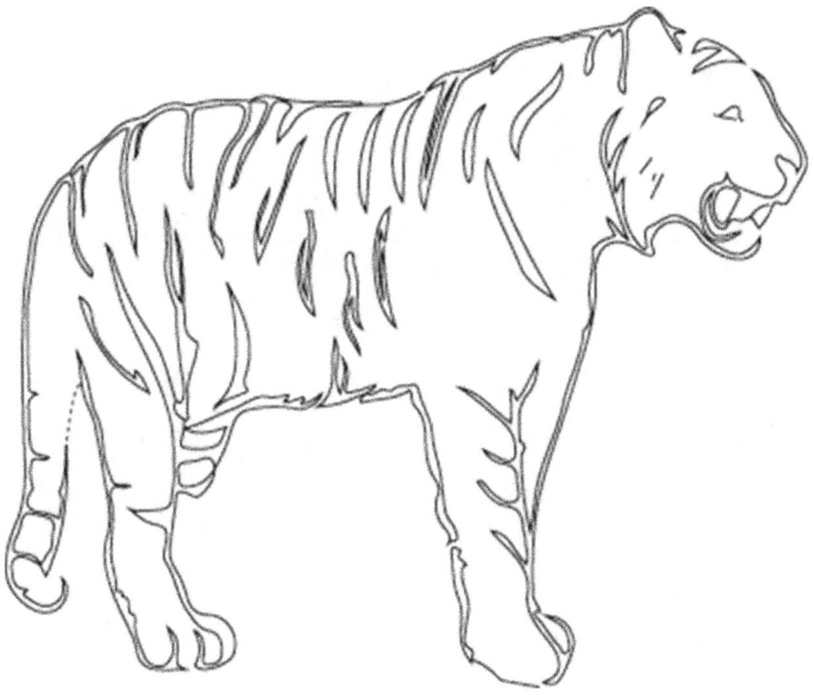

Tiger

TRYING AREA

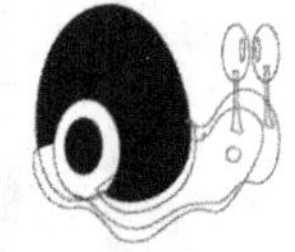

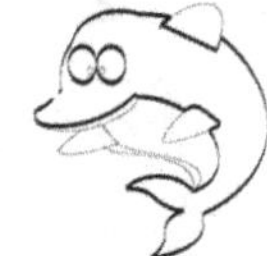

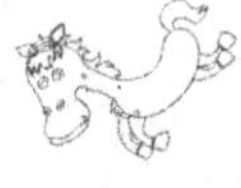

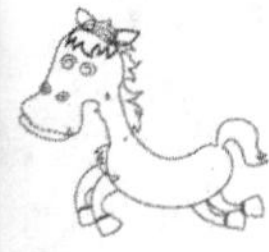
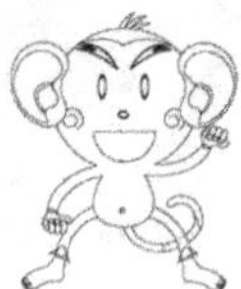
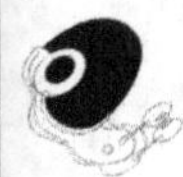
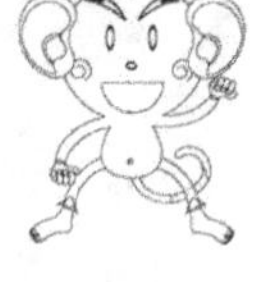
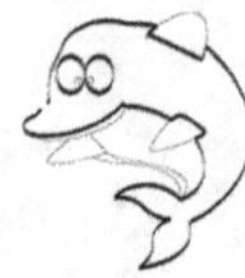
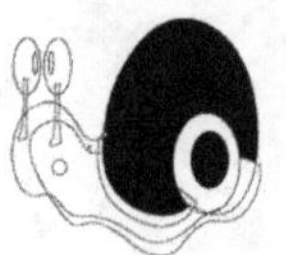

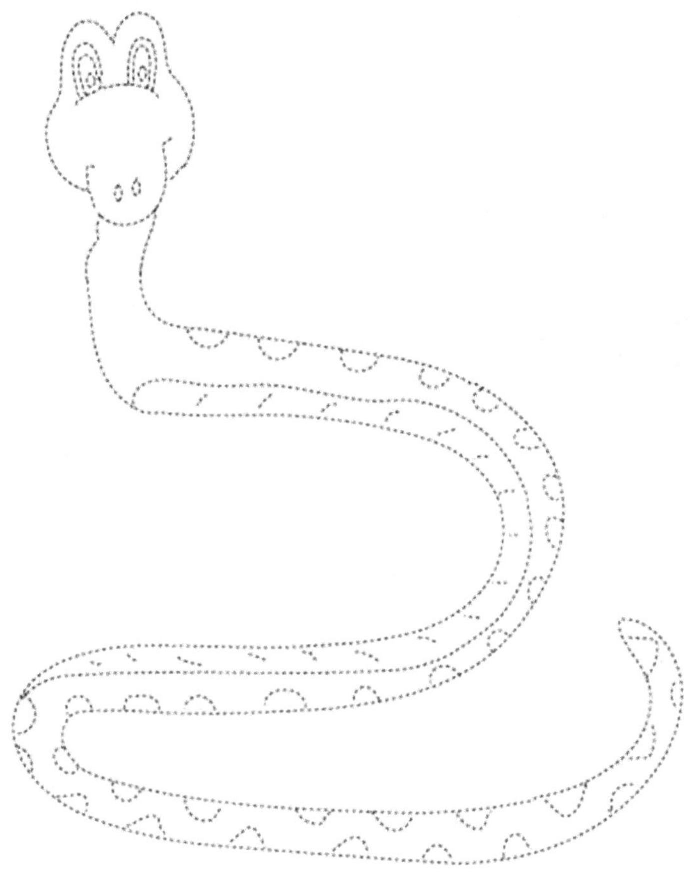

Snake

TRYING AREA

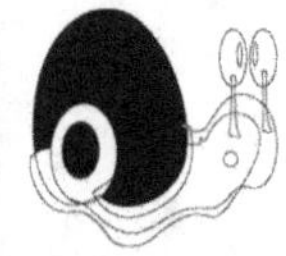

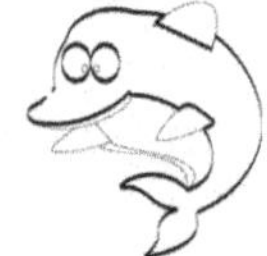

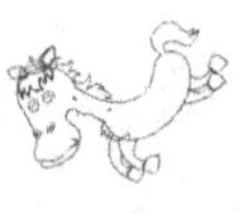
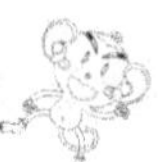

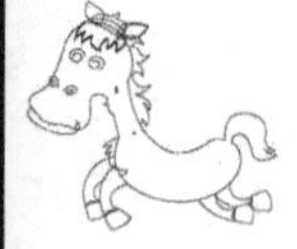
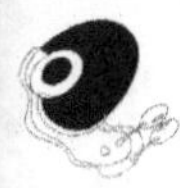
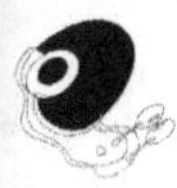
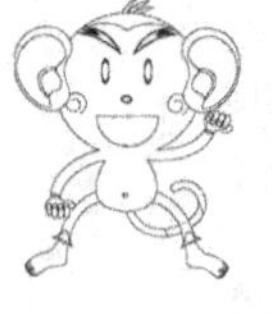
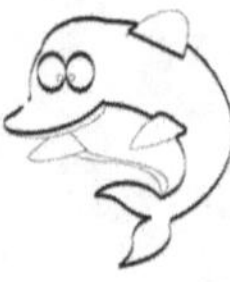
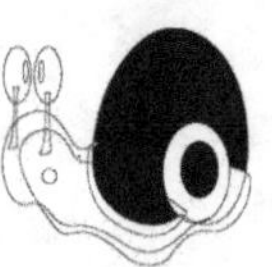

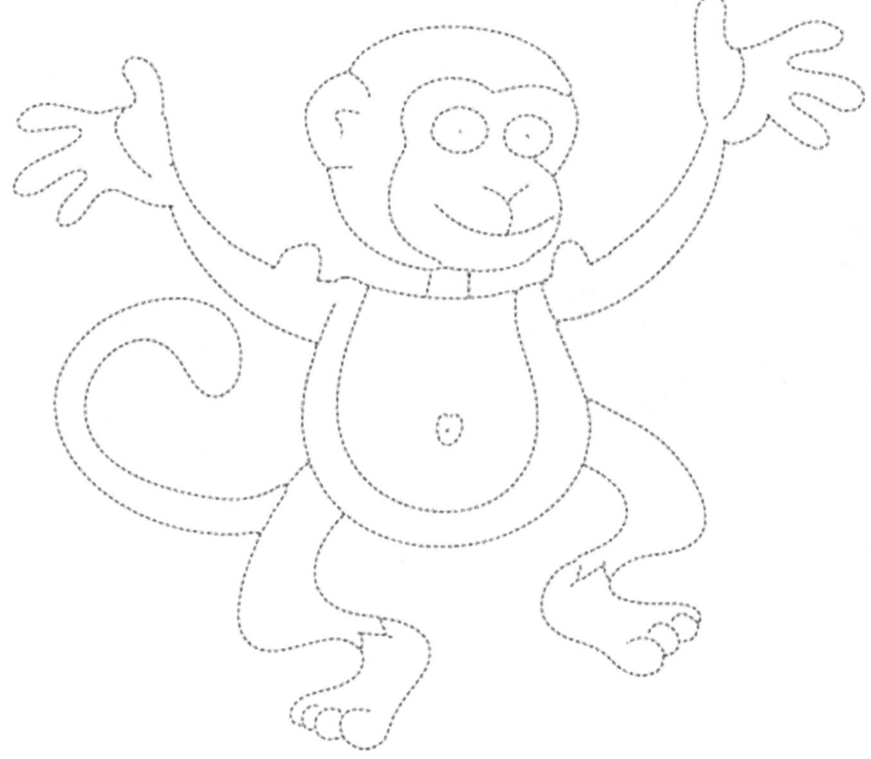

Monkey

TRYING AREA

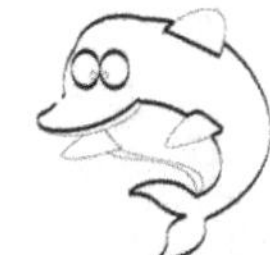

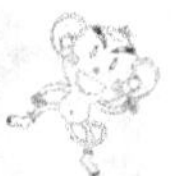
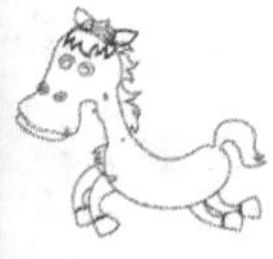
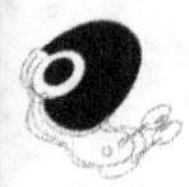
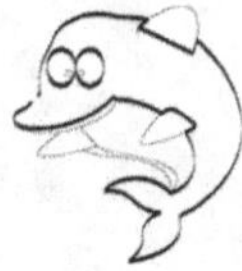
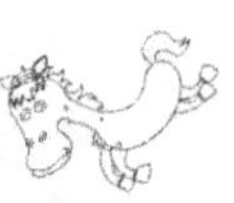

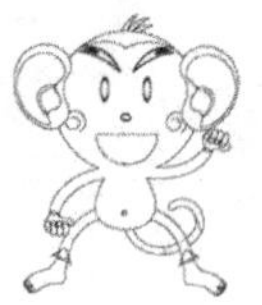
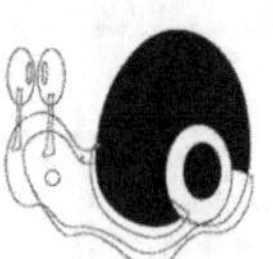